Contents

Symbols

+	check
!!	brilliant move
!	good move
!?	interesting move
?!	dubious move
?	bad move
??	blunder
1-0	The game ends in a win for White
0-1	The game ends in a win for Black
½-½	The game ends in a draw

Introduction

The study of chess openings is difficult and never-ending. It's like Pandora's box: the more you study, the more there is to learn; and the more you learn, the more you realize how little you know. If that's the opinion of someone who's been trying for nearly 30 years to get to grips with openings, how does a newcomer to chess find this ever-spiralling science? Intimidating, or is that too mild a description?

So what is an aspiring player supposed to do? Although not strictly relevant here, I can't help but be reminded of one of Bobby Fischer's famous quotes. On being quizzed over chess lessons, Bobby Fischer advised his biographer and founding editor of Chess Life magazine, Frank Brady, (tongue-in-cheek, I'm sure): 'For the first lesson, I want you to play over every column of Modern Chess Openings, including the footnotes. And for the next lesson, I want you to do it again.' Of course it goes without saying that opening encyclopaedias are an important part of chess literature, but I do wonder how I would have found the experience as a junior player of ploughing through the latest volume of intense opening theory. A bit bewildering, perhaps?

This book is a bit different and is mainly aimed at those who know nothing or very little about chess openings. It's also for those who do know some moves of opening theory, who have happily played these moves in their own games, but are perhaps not quite sure why they play them! One of my main aims was to give the reader enough confidence to face the unknown; to be able to play good, logical moves in the opening despite in many cases having a lack of concrete knowledge of the theory. After all, even in grandmaster games there comes a point when one or both players runs out of theory and has to rely on general opening principles, and sometimes this is sooner than you would think.

The initial inspiration behind Discovering Chess Openings stemmed from coaching sessions I did with some young students not experienced enough to have any real knowledge of opening theory. After revising the basic principles of opening play, I decided as exercises to give them a number of positions from typical openings, often only three or four moves deep into the game. I then let them spend some time finding logical moves and, in turn, appropriate replies to these moves. The idea was to find out how players with little or no knowledge of opening theory but with some understanding of general opening principles would fare when confronted with an opening position they knew nothing about.

This concept really appealed to me. The traditional approach had been to carefully go through the mainline openings, taking measures to explain the reasoning behind each move, but somehow it seemed so much more beneficial (not to mention more fun!) to watch the students trying to work out the best moves of their own accord; basically, trying to recreate opening theory! It was fascinating to revisit well known positions with players whose views were not influenced by previous knowledge; this definitely brought a certain freshness to their ideas. On the other hand, some suggestions that were made did reinforce one or two common misconceptions amongst improving players, and I've included these in the book to emphasize what we should be particularly looking out for.

This book has also given me the opportunity to expand on a number of topics which arose when I was writing Concise Chess, a general guide for absolute beginners. These themes were too advanced for that book, so I was happy to be able to include them in a more suitable place.

Finally, a brief paragraph about how the book was written and what it contains. The first three chapters introduce the three main ideas behind opening play:

1) Control of the centre
2) Rapid piece development
3) King safety.

There are other important concepts, but as far as I can see these are usually just sub-sets of these three. Chapters 4 and 5 delve more deeply into these themes, with the latter chapter concentrating on the role pawns play in the opening. Finally, in Chapter 6 we take all the ideas of the previous chapters and see how they are used to create modern opening theory.

Whilst many mainline openings can be found within these pages, not everything under the sun is covered. As I've already mentioned, it was never the intention to be encyclopaedic. Perhaps I've indulged a little more in 1 e4 e5 openings, and if so I make no excuses for this. In my experience, these are the first openings that many newcomers learn, so they are likely to come across these more frequently than other openings in the initial stages of their development.

I think I've said enough. I hope you enjoy this book and wish you the best of luck discovering chess openings!

John Emms,
Kent, July 2006

Chapter One

Central Issues

What is 'the centre'? Okay, I admit this sounds a silly question, but even so I'd be happier if I were able to confirm one or two definitions here. 'The centre' is very often considered to be simply the four squares highlighted in the diagram below: e4, d4, e5 and d5.

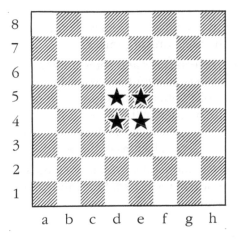

This definition, however, has always seemed a bit restrictive to me. I think you lose something if you say these four squares are the centre, everything else isn't; I don't think it's as black and white as that (excuse the pun!). For this book's purposes I'd like to expand the centre a little to include the squares c4, c5, f4, f5, d3, e3, d6 and e6 (see the following diagram).

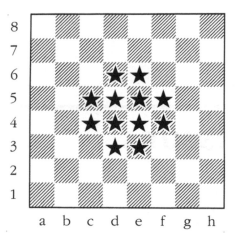

I'd be the first to admit that these extra eight squares aren't quite as important as e4, d4, e5 and d5, but they still carry some significance and so I think it's right to include them here.

Why is it important to pay attention to the centre? Why not ignore the centre and play only on the flanks?

Good questions! One or two further answers will crop up later on in the book, but for now I'd like to give the following arguments:

1) Let's use an analogy between chess and some other sports and games (chess has been described as many things; just for the record, I would classify it as a mind sport). In soccer, for example, I often hear commentators using phrases such as, 'Control the midfield and you control the game.' Something similar could easily be used to describe a game of chess. For one thing, if you control the centre then it should be easier for you to access all sides of the board.

2) Chess pieces are generally more powerful, more mobile and thus more influential when placed in the centre of the board. Put simply, they are able to control more squares from the centre.

Piece Mobility

I think the second point is best illustrated by using the example of the knight. Let's place it in the centre of an empty board, say on the e4-square.

(see following diagram)

On e4 the knight is controlling eight squares; it's performing to its maximum capabilities.

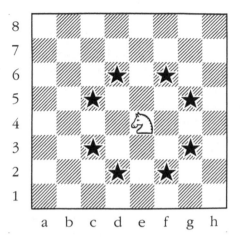

Now let's see what happens when the knight is placed on the edge of the board as in the next diagram.

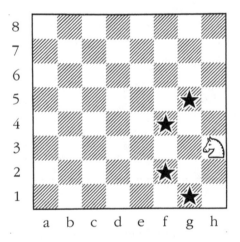

On this occasion, instead of eight squares the knight controls just four: g1, f2, f4 and g5. You could say that the knight is only playing to half of its full potential. The knight's reduced power on the edge of the board has led to the well-known and probably overused adage: 'Knight on the rim is dim!' (Some annotators replace 'dim' with 'grim', but you get the picture.) I've learned, sometimes from painful experience, that it's often very dangerous to generalize in chess – there are some occasions where a knight performs a heroic job on the edge of the board – but even so this is a guideline that's worth remembering.

Question: Where on the board does the knight control the fewest squares?

Answer: Perhaps unsurprisingly, in the corners of the board (a1, a8, h1 and h8). For example, a knight on h1 controls only two squares: f2 and g3. It could be said that here the knight is performing to only a quarter of its capabilities.

I should point out that the difference in mobility isn't as dramatic when we are talking about the long-range pieces: the queen, the bishop and the rook. For example, on the e4-square the queen controls 27 squares on an empty board; in any of the four corners this number is 21. This is only a 22% reduction in mobility, comparing very favourably with the knight's 75%.

Question: Which piece has the same mobility regardless of its placing on an empty board?

Answer: The rook: it controls 14 squares whether in the centre, on the edge or in the corner.

Just staying on the subject of piece mobility a little while longer, I recall when I was much younger being shown the following position, one that made a lasting impression on me:

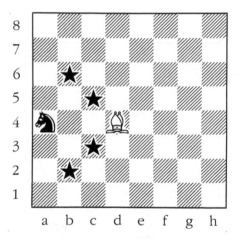

Black's knight cannot move without being captured; it's totally dominated by the bishop on d4. I remember former British Champion Chris Ward using the term 'corralling' here, which I think sums it up quite nicely.

Let's try switching the pieces around.

(see following diagram)

The bishop still prevents the knight from moving safely to four squares, but because the knight is in the middle of the board it has four other squares available: e6, f5, f3 and e2. You could even say that the knight dominates the bishop more than the bishop dominates the knight: the bishop only has three safe squares in d1, d7 and e8.

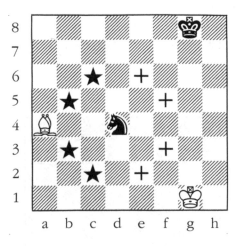

Question: If on the first move of a game White wanted to develop the g1-knight, which square would be most appropriate: f3 or h3?

Answer: 1 Nf3! is much stronger than 1 Nh3.

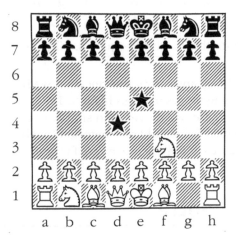

On f3 the knight controls eight squares in total. Not only that; two of these are the central squares d4 and e5. In contrast, 1 Nh3 would leave the knight controlling four squares, of which only f4 is central. The value of the move 1 Nf3 is underlined by its popularity: according to my database 1 Nf3 is the third most popular opening move for White.

Controlling the Centre: The Easy Guide

The quickest and easiest way to battle for control of the centre from the start of the game is by placing pawns in the middle.

Question: Can you suggest any opening pawn move for White that controls two central squares?

Answer: By playing 1 e4!...

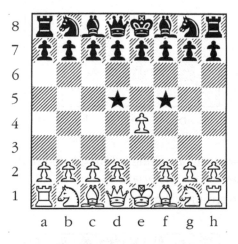

...White stakes a claim for the d5- and f5-squares. Likewise, after 1 d4! the pawn controls both e5 and c5.

Progress has been made! By answering this question we have 'discovered' White's two most popular opening moves in chess history: 1 e4! and 1 d4!. I should point out that there's more to these two moves than simply to control the centre, but more about that in Chapter 2. I should also mention that both 1 e3 and 1 d3 also control two central squares, but these moves are far less popular because they gain less space.

The Classical Centre

Question: If White were allowed to make two unopposed moves at the beginning of the game, what would be a good option?

Answer: 1 e4! followed by 2 d4!, or 1 d4! followed by 2 e4!.

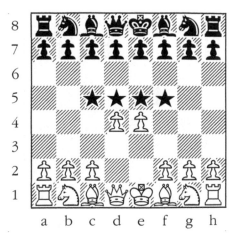

With these two moves White has staked a claim for the squares c5, d5, e5 and f5; he is well on the way to central domination! This ideal formation for White is known as the 'classical centre'.

Preventing the Classical Centre

Okay, this is all well and good, but of course Black is also playing the game and is allowed to have a move in between. Let's say White plays the opening move 1 e4 (I think it's time to stop adorning this and 1 d4 with an exclamation mark – I think you've already guessed that I like them).

Question: Given the assumption that White wants to play the move 2 d4 to create the ideal centre, and Black cannot physically prevent this, are there any moves that Black can play that will disrupt White's 'ideal centre'?

Answer: Yes! Black needs to be in a position to capture either the e4- or d4-pawn on his second move. Black could get ready to capture the pawn on d4 with 1...e5 or 1...c5 (this would be a trade as White's queen could recapture) or alternatively he could attack the undefended e4-pawn with 1...d5, 1...f5 or 1...Nf6.

More discoveries: the moves 1...e5, 1...c5, 1...d5 and 1...Nf6 are all perfectly good opening replies to 1 e4, and are seen in countless games at all levels. The only move you're very unlikely to spot a grandmaster playing is 1...f5?, which loses a pawn to 2 exf5 and weakens the black king (I'll chat more about the problem of the f-pawn later).

I think it's time to name one opening, and we might as well start at the very top. Let's look at the position after 1...c5.

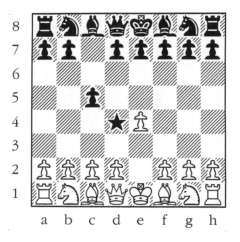

1...c5 is known as the Sicilian Defence, or – especially by ambitious players who don't believe in 'defending' with Black – simply the Sicilian. This is the most widely-played opening, one that even many non-chessplayers have heard of.

Exercises

1) According to my definitions in this chapter, how many central squares are there?

2) How many squares does a knight control from (a) c2, (b) e3 and (c) h4.

3) Can you think of three opening moves for White which control the square d5?

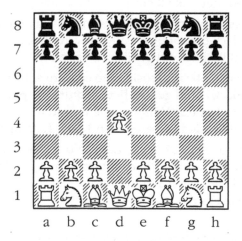

4) After the opening move **1 d4** (see the diagram), can you think of three moves that Black could play to prevent White from setting up the ideal centre with 2 e2-e4?

Chapter Two

Introducing Development

I think we'll begin with another clarification: in chess, 'development' is the term used for the process of bringing your pieces into play from their initial positions on the back rank. So if White plays the move 1 Nc3...

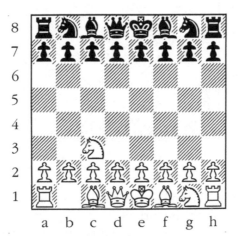

...he is 'developing' this knight, bringing it into play. Chess writers are constantly using the terms 'develop' and 'development' when describing events in the opening phase of the game. For example, if White has more pieces and pawns in play than Black has, then White is said to be 'ahead in development', and perhaps Black will be trying to 'catch up in development'.

Develop Rapidly!

Because of the way the pieces stand in the initial position, neither side is ready to lunge into an immediate attack. Apart from the knights, which have the advantage of being able to jump, all the pieces are hemmed in and held back behind the row of pawns; at least one or two of these pawns need to be moved to allow the powerful pieces out.

More than anything, it is common sense to develop most of your pieces as quickly as possible – you can hardly expect to be successful attacking with just one or two pieces while the rest of your army is still asleep in bed. Quantity matters here: in most cases it's better to outnumber than to be outnumbered. But quality matters too; in fact one of the main challenges facing a player in the opening is deciding on which squares his pieces will be best placed.

Another Good Reason for 1 e4 and 1 d4

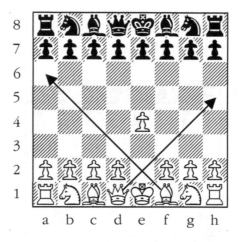

In the previous chapter we looked at one positive feature of the opening move 1 e4: the pawn on e4 controls the important central squares d5 and f5. There is, however, an even more apparent benefit to this pawn move: it clears the way for two pieces to move. Both White's queen and light-squared bishop now have available quite a few different squares on which they could be developed.

(see following diagram)

1 d4 is similar in that it allows both the dark-squared bishop and the queen to develop, although notice here that the queen has fewer options than after 1 e4.

I almost forgot to mention that with 1 e4 or 1 d4 White also creates the option of moving his king. This possibility, however, is more or less incidental. As we'll see later, moving the king out into the open so early is not to be advised!

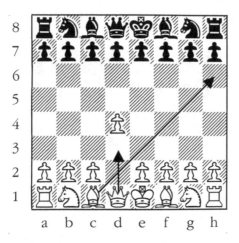

Checkmating in Four Moves!

My dad taught me the chess moves at quite an early age (I was five or six I think). One of the very first things he showed me was how to checkmate my opponent in only four moves. I remember being incredibly impressed by this revelation and couldn't wait to try out this idea against the other players at the school chess club, confident that it would lead to some easy wins. Sure enough, there was simply no answer and I racked up game after game. It was almost getting tedious. Almost, but not quite; like all newcomers addicted to the game, I was never bored by winning.

Here's how I would checkmate my unwary opponents:

1 e4 e5

1...e5 was mentioned in Chapter 1 as a way of preventing White from setting up the ideal centre with pawns abreast on e4 and d4 – if White plays a pawn to d4 Black will now be able to capture it. Furthermore, just like 1 e4 for White, it allows Black to develop both his queen and his f8-bishop. In fact, 1...e5 is a very popular reply to 1 e4 at all levels of chess, and especially amongst those new to the game.

2 Qh5

(see following diagram)

No messing about: 1 e4 allowed the queen to develop so why hesitate? What's more, White already has a threat: capturing the pawn on e5.

Question: Assuming the players are adhering to the rules of competitive chess (touch move: if a piece is touched it must be moved), which piece would Black want to avoid touching here?

Answer: The king! The only move that Black could play is 2...Ke7 but this allows an immediate mate with 3 Qxe5 – one move earlier than planned!

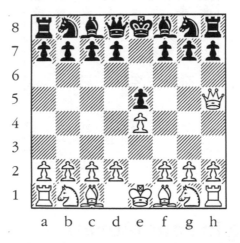

Attacking the white queen with 2...g6? doesn't allow a mate in one but is almost as disastrous. Following 3 Qxe5+ White's queen forks the king and rook, capturing the rook after Black gets out of check.

2...Nc6!

A good move, both developing a piece and defending the e5-pawn.

3 Bc4

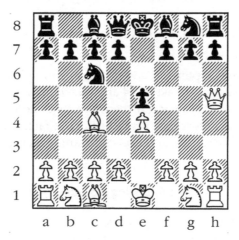

This is another move that makes good use of 1 e4. The bishop was free to develop so why not?

Now comes the moment of truth. At this stage when playing with the white pieces it's advisable to adopt your best 'poker face'.

3...Nf6??

With the threat to the e5-pawn averted, it's time to get rid of that pesky queen! Or so thought most of my early opponents...

4 Qxf7 mate!

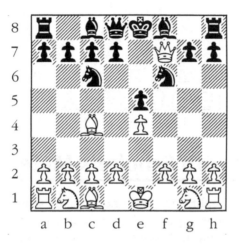

Checkmate! White's previous move (3 Bc4) introduced a new threat to Black's f7-pawn – it was attacked twice and only defended once – and 3...Nf6?? did nothing to counter this threat. Unbeknown to me at the time, my dad hadn't come up with some earth-shattering new invention: this checkmating plan is known as scholar's mate and is one of the first ideas that newcomers to the game learn.

A Remedy to Scholar's Mate

I can't remember exactly how long I was in blissful ignorance, thinking that there was absolutely no way to prevent scholar's mate, but one day my dad demonstrated a remedy.

1 e4 e5 2 Qh5 Nc6 3 Bc4 g6!

(see following diagram)

It was as simple as that. The pawn on g6 blocks the queen's path to f7 and checkmate is successfully averted. How had I missed that idea? But there was more: Black had other good ways to avoid being mated.

Question: Can you spot three more ways of defending against scholar's mate? On each occasion Black defends the f7-pawn.

Answer: As well as 3...g6, Black can play 3...Qf6, 3...Qe7 or 3...Nh6.

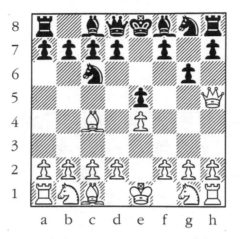

The Problem with Scholar's Mate

Okay, perhaps I should rephrase this: it's not actually scholar's mate that's the problem (checkmating your opponent in four moves is a nice problem to have); it's what happens when you start coming up against players who either know the checkmating idea or are good enough to work out a defence over the board.

There's a negative aspect to White's crude attack, and this becomes more apparent when taking a closer look. Let's go over the opening moves again, and see what could happen if Black defended against the initial mating threat.

1 e4 e5 2 Qh5 Nc6 3 Bc4 g6!

3...Qe7, 3...Qf6 and 3...Nh6 are all possible defences, but I prefer this move because not only does it prevent the checkmate, it also attacks the white queen and thus forces it to move. Is that a good thing? Let's see...

4 Qf3!

This square is the best place to retreat the queen. Now for a second time Black is faced with the threat of Qxf7 mate.

4...Nf6!

(see following diagram)

I really like this move: Black blocks the threat and at the same time develops his other knight. Now if White were being sensible, he would adopt the attitude of, 'Okay, Black has prevented my two tricky mate threats; let's begin getting some more pieces into the game' and play 5 Ne2, but let's see what happens if White goes 'checkmate crazy'...

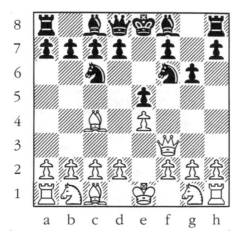

5 g4??

White is unrelenting in his assault of the f7-pawn: he wants to play g4-g5 in order to remove the knight from blocking the f-file. Surely it's now up to Black to deal with this threat, but White is in for a shock...

5...Nd4!

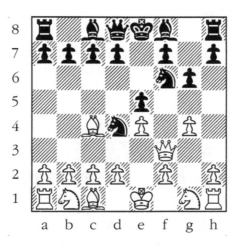

Another attack on the white queen, but this time it's far more serious as there is an additional threat of....Nxc2+, forking the king and rook and thus winning the rook in the corner.

6 Qd1

Moving the queen out of attack and defending the c2-pawn. White's queen is not having so much fun anymore!

Question: White could also defend the c2-pawn with 6 Qd3. What could Black play against this?

Answer: Black could simply win a pawn with 6...Nxg4!.

6...d5!

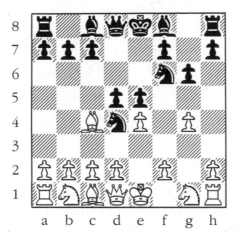

Now it's Black who's beginning to create all the threats: both the bishop on c4 and the pawn on e4 are attacked.

7 exd5

This capture is an obvious solution to the double threat posed by Black's previous move, but there was one further point behind the multi-purpose idea 6...d5. Can you spot it?

7...Bxg4!

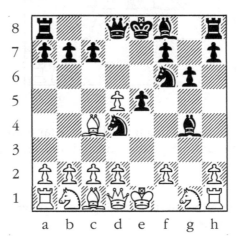

Exactly! Moving the d-pawn unleashed the c8-bishop. Now this piece introduces itself to the action in no uncertain terms, grabbing a pawn and making yet another threat on White's queen, who's beginning to feel just a little bit harassed.

8 Ne2??

White's queen actually had no safe squares to go to, so a block was the only way to deal with the threat. Unfortunately for White, he chooses the wrong one.

8...Nf3+!

Black's fourth consecutive threat (given that checking is a special kind of threat that cannot be ignored).

9 Kf1 Bh3 mate!

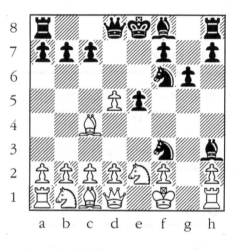

Amazing – the game ends abruptly, but it's Black who ends up checkmating White. This position is far removed from the one where it was White threatening mate on f7, but actually this was only five moves ago!

So where did this game go so horribly pear-shaped for White? It all started so brightly with two mate threats in a row but then Black suddenly stepped up a gear, created four consecutive threats himself and then delivered a snap mate.

White's downfall can be traced back to how he managed his queen. Basically, it made three moves in the game and finally ended up back on its original square; one could justifiably call this a waste of three moves! Because of this loss of time, White quickly lost the initiative and Black stormed ahead in development.

The problem was that White's queen was forced to move twice because it was attacked by black pieces of lesser value – on each occasion Black gained time because of this. And there lies the problem with developing the queen so early: the further advanced the queen becomes, the more prone it is to attack from enemy pieces, and this is particularly the case in the opening when there have been no piece trades and the board is cluttered. If you're not careful with your queen handling in the opening then you could easily lose time as it gets pushed from pillar to post. And losing time is not a good idea because you are likely to fall behind in development.

Okay, I must admit that it wasn't just the early queen raid that led to White's catastrophic demise here. Perhaps trying to emphasize the point a bit too much, I did help White along the way with a couple of horrible mistakes. 8 Ne2??, allowing mate in two, could of course have been improved upon (8 f3!), although it's fair to say much of the damage had been done by then. However, the real blunder that turned the tide was 5 g4??, which was consistent with White's attack on f7 but paid no heed whatsoever to what Black was threatening. Instead White should have safeguarded his queen's position to some extent with the move 5 Ne2!, preparing to meet....Nd4 with a trade of knights.

Points to Remember

1) Handle your queen with great care in the opening. You don't want to be in a position where your opponent keeps gaining time simply by repeatedly attacking your queen.

2) Always check to see if your opponent's previous move threatens anything. Of course this applies to every stage of the game, not just the opening.

Slowcoach Rooks

Perhaps because of my rapid introduction and deadly attraction to scholar's mate, I never really felt enticed by the thought of developing my rooks as quickly as possible in the opening. Many newcomers to the game, however, seem to be attracted more by the rook than any other piece. Maybe it's because, with their relatively simple up-and-down/side-to-side movements, beginners feel very much at ease with rooks. In turn, they are very keen to introduce rooks quickly into the game. The problem is, however, there is no easy way to do this. I lost count of the number of times my early games began something like this:

1 a4?

Seemingly the easiest way to activate the a1-rook, but it's not that simple...

1...e5

A clever move, spotting White's 'threat'.

2 Ra3??

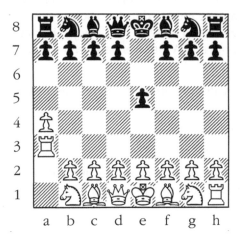

2...Bxa3!

Oops. Watch out for those tricky bishops.

3 bxa3 d5 4 h4

Has White learned his lesson?

4...Nf6 5 Rh3??

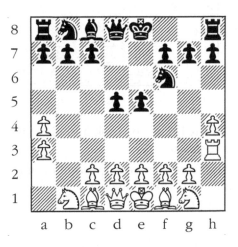

No!

5...Bxh3! 6 gxh3

...and, having been presented with two rooks in exchange for two bishops – a healthy four point swing – I was obviously in a good mood for the rest of the game.

This, however, is only telling half the story. I wouldn't want to give you the impression that it's only a poor idea to develop rooks as soon as possible in this way if your opponent covers h3 and a3 with his bishops; in fact it's a poor idea, period. Let's see what could happen if White were allowed to carry out his wish:

1 a4? d5

Did Black miss a trick by not playing 1...e5 here? Not really.

2 Ra3?

Objective achieved, but...

2...e5!

One move later than in the previous example, but still very effective. Now White is forced to move the rook again. Is this a good thing? Let's see.

3 Re3

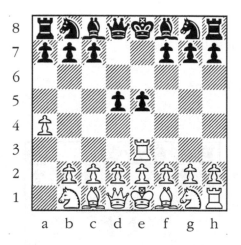

Seemingly very logical: White brings the rook into play (into the centre) and gains time by attacking Black's e-pawn.

Objectively speaking, White's best move is to admit his mistake and tuck the rook back into the corner with 3 Ra1! That, however, is not quite as much fun as the text continuation; fun for Black that is.

3...Nc6

Defending e5 and developing a knight – all good stuff.

4 Nf3

And White keeps up the pressure on the e5-pawn.

4...d4!

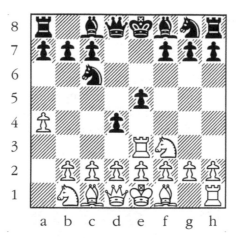

The first sign that all is not so happy in the white camp: the rook is attacked and its options are somewhat limited.

5 Rb3

After this move Black can begin to push White's pieces from pillar to post, but it's pretty much the same story if White tries other rook moves: 5 Rd3 falls fouls of the simple fork 5...e4! winning a knight, while 5 Rxe5+ Nxe5 6 Nxe5 is a good trade points-wise for Black. The rook is certainly centralized after 5 Re4, and the threat to the e5-pawn remains, but 5...Bf5! 6 Rh4 Be7! 7 Rh5 g6! sees the rook run out of safe squares; the best it can do is to give itself up for the bishop after 8 Rxf5 gxf5.

5...e4!

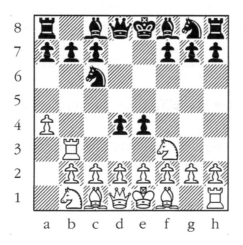

Why not? The knight's retreat looks rather sad.

6 Ng1 Be6!

Offering White the chance to grab a pawn on b7, but Black has spotted a clever way to trap White's rook.

7 Rxb7

After 7 Rg3 Black keeps up his relentless harassment with 7...Bd6! and following 8 Rxg7 Qf6! he is finally rewarded – the rook no longer has a safe square and is forced to give itself up. The continuation 7 Rb5 meets a similar fate: 7...a6 8 Rh5 (where else? 8 Rxb7 Na5 and the rook runs out of squares) 8...Nf6 9 Rh4 g5 is almost comical.

7...a6!

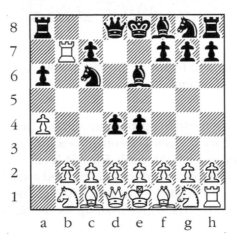

Covering the only available escape square for the rook.

Question: With the white rook lacking any safe squares, how will Black round it up on his next move?

Answer: Either 8...Qc8 or 8...Na5 will attack the rook and win material.

8 d3

Of course White has other possibilities but nothing that saves the rook.

8...Na5! 9 Rb3

The best of a bad job. At least this way White ends up with one of Black's minor pieces, but of course it's still a poor trade.

9...Nxb3 10 cxb3 Nf6

White's rook had an eventful if brief life, but in the end it was forced to sell itself rather cheaply and White's position is a bit of a wreck (I'm not sure that this would prevent a particularly stubborn rook junkie from playing 11 h4 intending Rh3).

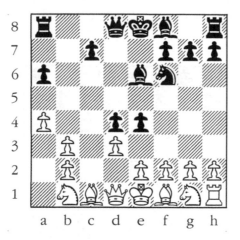

Before going any further, there is one point I think I should make about this example: the almost inevitable trapping and capture of White's rook should not be seen as the only refutation to White's opening strategy. Black has no need to go out of his way to trap the rook; just good, solid developing moves will be more than sufficient to refute White's play. For example, 6...Be6 7 Rxb7 a6! was a smart idea that required some calculation, but I don't think that anyone could really argue after the more mundane 6...Nf6 followed by developing the f8-bishop and castling kingside that White's opening has been nothing short of a disaster: he's completely overrun in the centre and falling way behind in development.

Point to Remember

Whereas rooks love open spaces and really come into their own in the endgame, they are notoriously slow starters; in fact they would prefer to have a good lie-in while the other pieces are busily developing. The rook hates roaming around the board in the opening stages of the game even more than the queen: just like the queen, the rook is vulnerable to attack from enemy pawns and minor pieces; however, with its relatively limited power, the rook finds it even more difficult to escape their attentions.

Minor Pieces and Pawns Rule!

We know that queens should be handled with great care early on, while it seems that rooks are almost allergic to the opening phase of the game. So what does that leave? By a process of elimination it could be said that the opening is reserved mainly for minor pieces and pawns to strut their stuff. For one thing, minor pieces and pawns are less likely to get harassed than the queen and rook. Because of their low value, an attack can often be ignored if the piece is already protected. For example:

1 d4 Nf6 2 Bg5

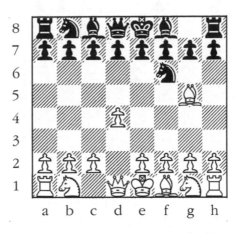

With White's second move he immediately attacks Black's only developed piece, the knight on f6. However, Black doesn't need to panic and move the knight since it is protected by both the e7- and g-pawns. As bishops and knights are roughly equal in value (three points each), Black has nothing really to fear over a trade on f6.

Likewise, if an attacked minor piece or pawn is unprotected, then it may be possible to defend it with another developing move rather than move it again and lose time:

1 e4 e6

This is the French Defence, another popular choice for Black. I'll cover it in more detail in Chapters 5 and 6.

2 d4 d5

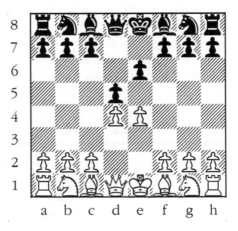

Black's move threatens to win a pawn with 3...dxe4. White has the option of moving the pawn with 3 e5, or trading pawns with 3 exd5, after which Black can choose to recapture with pawn or queen. However, there's also a third choice, incidentally White's most popular move here, which is to defend the pawn with a developing move.

3 Nc3

Now White is ready to recapture on e4 with the knight. Let's see what could happen if Black captured on e4.

3...dxe4 4 Nxe4 Bd7

Planning to attack the knight with ...Bc6.

5 Nf3 Bc6

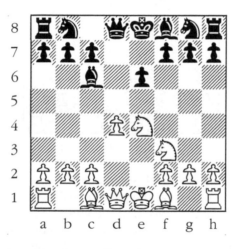

Now White's knight is under threat. One idea is to move the knight out of danger (say 6 Nc3 or Ng3). However, White also has the possibility of defending the knight whilst developing another piece with...

6 Bd3!

...effectively killing two birds with one stone. Given the similar value of knights and bishops, White isn't unhappy if Black decides to trade on e4 with 6...Bxe4 7 Bxe4, and White hasn't been forced to lose time which would have been the case after any knight move.

Okay, that seems like good, solid advice: put your pawns in the centre, develop your minor pieces and you can't go too far wrong. There's a bit more to it than that, however: the tricky part is knowing on which squares to place these pieces. More on this little problem soon.

Development Count

A useful marker to see how quickly each side is developing is to perform a development count. Each piece that is developed scores a point and I would also count pawn moves in the centre (they control the centre and allow easy development). Let's go back to a couple of positions we've recently visited. Taking the previous example after 6 Bd3:

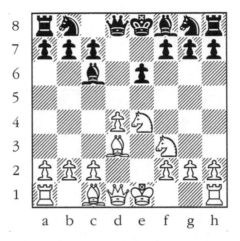

White's development count is four (three minor pieces and the pawn on d4), while Black's is two (the bishop on c6 and the pawn on e6), so it could be said that White is leading 4-2 in development. Notice that the knight on e4 and the bishop on c6 only score one point, even though both pieces have moved twice. Just because a piece has been moved twice doesn't mean to say it's going to be more effectively placed than one that's moved only once.

Let's go back to the example on page 28, arising after the moves

1 a4 d5 2 Ra3 e5 3 Re3 Nc6 4 Nf3 d4 5 Rb3 e4 6 Ng1 Be6 7 Rxb7 a6 8 d3 Na5 9 Rb3 Nxb3 10 cxb3 Nf6

(see following diagram)

Question: What are the development scores here?

Answer: Here Black has a development count of four (the e6-bishop, the f6-knight, plus the pawns on d4 and e4) whereas White scores only one (the pawn on d3).

So not only does Black have a material advantage, he also has a substantial development lead; added up this amounts to a major advantage.

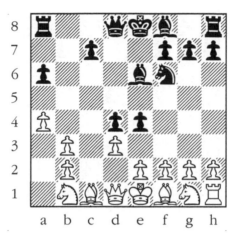

Notice here that the pawns on b3, a4 and a6 don't score because they contribute little or nothing towards development. White's knight on g1 has moved twice yet scores nothing because it has ended up back on its original square, while White's a1-rook has actually taken up half of White's moves but doesn't score as it's now off the board. In the final analysis, from White's angle a development score of one point from ten moves is a pretty poor showing!

Ideal Squares: The Knight

Now I'd like to talk a little bit about the ideal initial places to develop knights and bishops. This subject is a bit tricky because ideal squares will vary to some extent depending on the opening and, in particular, the pawn structure, but there are certainly some guidelines that are useful to know.

Rather than attempting to generalize over all possible openings, I think it would be easiest to look closely at one particular opening for the moment (1 e4 e5). Many principles here will remain with other openings, even if the actual squares in question differ.

We'll deal with knights first because on the whole its choice of development is less complex than the bishop's. We've noted previously that knights generally prefer the centre to the edge of the board, and this gives us a big clue to its favoured position.

Let's take the position after **1 e4 e5** and examine the three possibilities for the g1-knight in turn (we should bear in mind that White doesn't have to develop this knight immediately):

Ne2

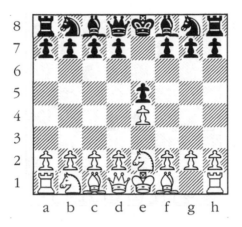

From e2 the knight controls six squares, including the central ones d4 and f4. It also supports the advances d2-d4 and f2-f4, both of which challenge Black's e5-pawn. From e2 the knight could continue its journey via c3, where it controls two central squares but takes away a developing option for the b1-knight, or g3 from where the knight eyes both f5 and h5.

A major worry that must be addressed is that on e2 the knight blocks the f1-bishop's development into the game. This problem could be solved in three ways: firstly, White could make sure he got the bishop developed along the f1-a6 diagonal before developing the knight; secondly, White could develop the bishop along a different diagonal by playing g2-g3 and then either Bg2 or Bh3; thirdly, White could move the knight again to either c3 or g3.

Nf3

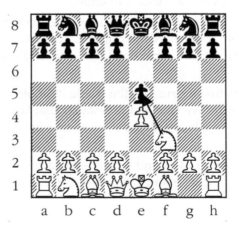

From here the knight controls eight squares, the maximum amount for a knight, and this includes the important central squares d4 and e5. The knight attacks Black's pawn on e5 and so gives Black an immediate problem to solve, while it also supports the pawn advance d2-d4. As well as attacking e5, there's the possibility in the future to play Nh4 and especially Ng5, which as we'll see later is an important attacking move (note, however, that both g5 and h4 are currently guarded by the black queen). The only real negative is that on f3, the knight blocks the possible pawn break f2-f4, but White could always consider playing f2-f4 before Nf3 (more about pawn breaks in Chapter 5).

Nh3

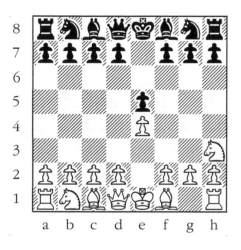

From h3 the knight controls only four squares. Only one of these (f4) is central, and this is less significant than the main four squares in the centre: d4, e4, d5 and e5. The knight does support the possible advance f2-f4 but does little else: it attacks nothing and its only real hope of getting into the game is via g5 or perhaps via f4; ...exf4; Nxf4 (this sounds okay in theory but in practice it's difficult to carry out).

Conclusion

With everything considered, the general guideline in 1 e4 e5 openings is that the best square for the knight is f3; the second best square for the knight is e2; and the third best square is h3. Using the mirror image to look at Black's situation, it's easy to deduce that the order of preference here is ...Nf6, ...Ne7 and ...Nh6.

A similar procedure could be performed for the b1-knight, although here it's not always so obvious that c3 is the best square. On many occasions the knight chooses d2 instead, the reason being that the c3-square is often occupied by the c-pawn, which plays a crucial role in supporting the central advance d4 (we'll talk more about this important theme later).

Ideal Squares: The Bishop

Looking at bishop moves in isolation is more difficult than with knight moves because it soon becomes clear that the ideal squares are more dependent on the placing of other pieces and pawns. Even so, I think it's still worth doing, as quite a few conclusions can be reached.

Let's take a look at the f1-bishop and its choices along the newly opened f1-a6 diagonal.

Be2

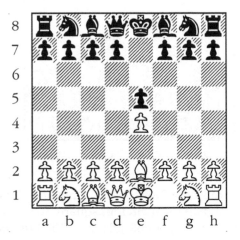

A safe, solid, if somewhat uninspiring position for the bishop. On e2 the bishop is well shielded from potential attack – being so far back it's unlikely to be harassed by enemy pieces. It's also useful defensively: it controls a few key squares on the kingside which could be important if White decides on kingside castling. On the other hand the bishop doesn't achieve that much in an attacking sense (you have to bear in mind that a knight may well be blocking its path along d1-h5 diagonal by standing on f3). If White plays the move d2-d3 – protecting the e4-pawn and preparing to develop the c1-bishop – then the light-squared bishop's path along f1-a6 diagonal is also blocked.

Bd3

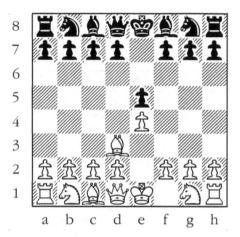

White has to be very careful about playing Bd3. In the diagrammed position – in fact in the vast majority of positions where White's d-pawn still stands on d2 – the move Bd3 is a big mistake because it blocks the d-pawn. White generally wishes to move the d-pawn fairly early on, both to influence the centre and, perhaps even more importantly, to allow the other bishop to develop along the c1-h6 diagonal. Thus a bishop on d3 really puts a spanner in the works, clogging up White's development.

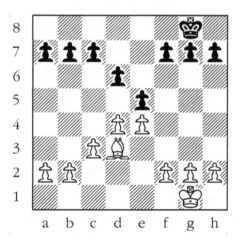

Things improve considerably if White has already played the move d2-d4, and in this case the bishop is reasonably well placed on d3 because it influences the centre, adding protection to the e4-pawn. It's true that the e4-pawn blocks the bishop's path along the b1-h7 diagonal. However, in the long term sometimes

Black's e5-pawn leaves the board – after, say, an exchange of pawns on d4 – and White is able to play the pawn advance e4-e5, unleashing the bishop's potential.

Bc4

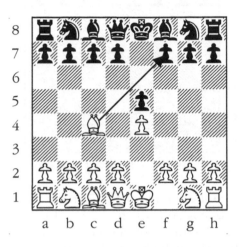

Just from a quick glance it's easy to see that in 1 e4 e5 openings the c4-square is a very attractive post for the bishop. From here the bishop controls two long diagonals, and the newly acquired one (a2-g8) looks a particular enticing prospect. The bishop adds extra control to the central square d5, while further down the diagonal it attacks the f7-pawn, a notorious weak point in Black's camp (we saw the vulnerability of f7 with scholar's mate and will examine it further in Chapter 3).

As the bishop travels further down the board it becomes more vulnerable to harassment from enemy pawns and pieces. Black could try to arrange the pawn moves ...b7-b5 or ...d7-d5 in order to attack the bishop. Note that ...d7-d5, for example, would need some preparation (perhaps ...c7-c6 and ...Nf6) because of White's control of d5.

Bb5

(see following diagram)

At first sight b5 seems to be a less attractive post for the bishop than c4, but in fact there's quite a lot going for this move, especially in the short term while Black's king remains on the e8-square. The point is that White can use the pressure along the a4-e8 diagonal in the battle to control the centre. In the diagram above, for example, where White has played the immediate 2 Bb5, Black's d-pawn is currently pinned to the king and so it cannot take any part in the battle. It should be said, though, that 2 Bb5 is not a particularly good move, since Black can reply 2...c6!

which gains time attacking the bishop and is a useful move in its own right – it supports a possible ...d7-d5 advance.

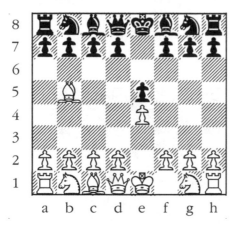

The move Bb5 is seen much more often once Black has committed his b8-knight to the c6-square. One of the most famous openings of all time, the Ruy Lopez, begins...

1 e4 e5 2 Nf3

We'll look at some theory behind 1 e4 e5 openings later on in the book, but I will just point out here that 2 Nf3 is White's most popular move. It's easy to see its plus points: a piece is developed, it creates a threat (an enemy pawn is attacked), and finally it prepares kingside castling (see Chapter 3).

2...Nc6

...And this is Black's most common reply. He too develops a piece and at the same time deals with the threat to the e5-pawn.

3 Bb5

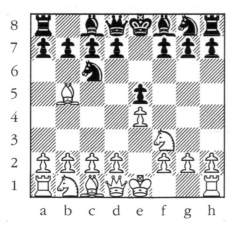

Here 3 Bb5 looks much more logical than the same move on the previous turn: 2 Nf3 created a threat by attacking the e5-pawn; 2...Nc6 developed a piece and at the same time defended the e5-pawn; and now 3 Bb5 attacks the knight which defends e5. Black must be wary of the pressure against e5, and another point of 3 Bb5 is seen if Black bolsters the e5-pawn with...

3...d6

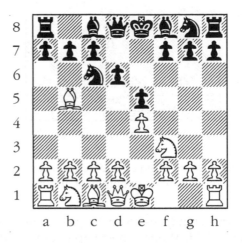

In this case the knight on c6 immediately becomes pinned to its own king and for the moment cannot play a part in the battle for the centre.

Conclusion

Normally the most desirable squares for the f1-bishop are c4 and b5: on c4 it bears down on Black's vulnerable f7 spot, while on b5 the bishop takes a very active role in the battle for the centre. The bishop is rarely good on d3 if White hasn't already moved the d-pawn, and on e2 the bishop is passively placed but useful for defensive purposes. Don't forget, we are only talking here about openings that arise after 1 e4 e5.

The Fianchetto

One further mode of development for the bishop that's worth pointing out (it occurs a few times in this book) is the so-called 'fianchetto', where the knight's pawn is moved and the bishop is developed in front of the knight.

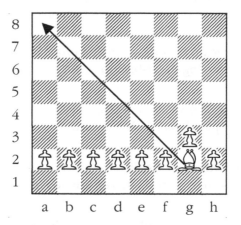

The diagram illustrates a typical fianchetto. The main attractions are that the bishop is actively placed, bears down on a long diagonal and covers two central squares (in this case e4 and d5). One disadvantage of the fianchetto is that it could be seen as a slightly 'slower' form of development: e2-e4 and g2-g3 both allow the bishop to be developed, but it's clear that e2-e4 has other benefits too (the queen can move out, for example), whereas moving the g-pawn only really helps the bishop.

Economic Development

I've already talked about the importance of developing quickly. In fact, this is reasonably easy to achieve so long as you stick to one or two guidelines.

Let's begin by looking at a very plausible sequence of opening moves.

1 d4 d5 2 Nf3 Nf6 3 e3

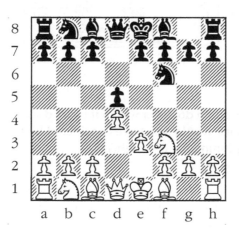

Question: White's previous move prepared to develop the f1-bishop, but at the same time blocked the route of the c1-bishop. Can you see a way round this problem?

Answer: White could develop the c1-bishop first (via 3 Bf4 or 3 Bg5) and only then play e2-e3 followed by moving the f1-bishop.

3...e6

Black follows suit. Going back to the previous question and answer, there was a strong argument here to play either 3...Bf5 or 3...Bg4.

4 c4

The pawn lunge c2-c4 occurs very frequently in 1 d4 d5 openings; we'll see why in Chapter 5. If Black takes on c4 then White is ready to recapture with the f1-bishop.

4...c6

Very solid! If White captures on d5, Black now has the extra option of recapturing with the c6-pawn. Black certainly has other moves here: he could develop his f8-bishop or challenge the centre with 4...c5.

5 Nc3

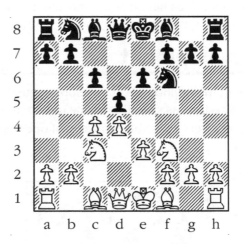

5...Bd6

The bishop is well placed on d6, from where it bears down on the b8-h2 diagonal. That said, certainly Black would also have considered both 5...Be7 (solid but a bit passive) and 5...Bb4 (pinning the c3-knight).

6 Qc2 Nbd7 7 Bd3 Bb4?

Black changes his mind and decides that the bishop should go to b4 in any case. Now is not the time to debate whether b4 is indeed a better square for the bishop than d6, but even if it is, isn't there something seriously wrong with Black's thinking here?

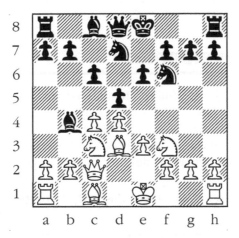

The truth is that Black has lost a valuable tempo with his indecision, an extra move that could have been put to very good use (castling, for instance). It would have been far better on move five to decide once and for all on which square the bishop should be deployed. And if Black were still uncertain at that juncture over the future of the bishop, it would have been better to play a move he was more sure about, like 5...Nbd7 (given that with the knight's choice of d7 and a6, there's only one winner).

By moving the bishop twice in the opening, Black has fallen behind in development (the count is 7-6 to White, who has the move). Not a significant loss, but an avoidable one all the same.

Points to Remember

1) Unless you are forced to, only develop a piece once you are sure you know the best place for it; if you are unsure, it is often wise to leave this piece alone and develop another piece whose best position you are more sure about.

2) Do not move a piece twice in the early stages of the game without good reason ('good reasons' will be discussed in Chapter 4).

Something that has been written endless times in chess opening literature is the guideline 'knights before bishops'. Really this piece of advice is simply a continuation of the first conclusion above. The point is that it's usually more immediately obvious where the knights want to go, whereas the bishops have more choice and their ideal posts may only become apparent later on.

I have to point out now and again that, as with much of what is said in this book, I'm talking about guidelines rather than hard and fast rules. If your opponent leaves his queen en prise to your bishop, the 'knights before bishops' argument should be quite low down on the list of priorities!

The 'Ideal' Development

Just for a bit of fun, imagine if White were allowed ten unanswered moves at the beginning of the game: what would he do? Okay, 1 e4, 2 Bc4, 3 Qh5 and 4 Qxf7 mate would be a good answer (!), but say White could only move each piece once and wasn't allowed to make any direct threats. If you asked this question to some strong chess players, their answers might differ very slightly, but most would put forward something like this:

1 e4 2 d4 3 Nf3 4 Nc3 5 Bc4 6 0-0 7 Bg5 8 Qe2 9 Rad1 10 Rfe1

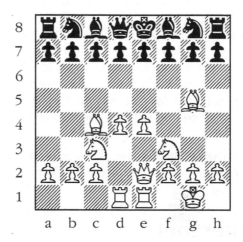

I can't quite remember where I first saw this type of set-up; maybe it was in one of Fred Reinfeld's books (Reinfeld was an incredibly prolific chess writer from New York with more than 100 books to his name). The diagram above shows an idealistic development by White, although this is one of a few possible set-ups – taste comes into it somewhere (some may prefer the dark-squared bishop on f4 for added symmetry!). What's clear is that White has a good pawn centre, his pieces are placed pretty much on their so-called best squares, and his king is tucked away safely on the kingside (more about this final point in the following chapter). Of course in a real game Black makes moves too, and it's unusual – though not exceptional – for Black to allow White such freedom of movement.

Exercises

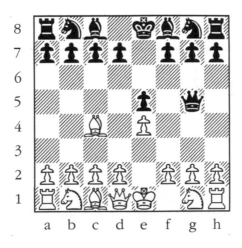

1) Here Black has gone for an immediate queen development with **1 e4 e5 2 Bc4 Qg5**, attacking White's g-pawn. What should White do?

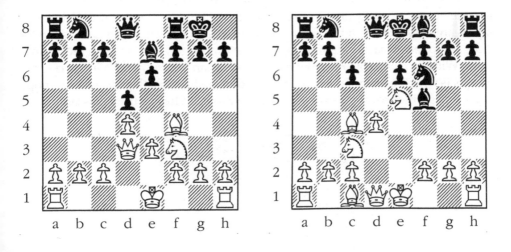

2) The two diagrams above were reached after the opening moves **1 d4 Nf6 2 Bg5 Ne4 3 Bf4 d5 4 Nd2 Bf5 5 e3 e6 6 Nxe4 Bxe4 7 Nf3 Be7 8 Bd3 Bxd3 9 Qxd3 0-0** and **1 e4 d5 2 exd5 Qxd5 3 Nc3 Qd8 4 d4 Nf6 5 Nf3 Bf5 6 Bc4 c6 7 Ne5 e6**. What are the development counts here?

Chapter Three

King Safety

Given that checkmate is the ultimate aim, king safety is always of paramount importance, and this applies to the opening just as it does to other phases of the game.

The Castled King

The obvious way of trying to ensure king safety in the opening is to castle (usually kingside but occasionally on the queenside). In the fight for central control, both players are very likely to advance one or more of their central pawns early on in the game, and often at least one pair disappears in exchanges, leaving open files in the centre. With no pawn cover in front of it, the king can feel vulnerable in the centre, and this is why it usually prefers to castle and move towards the side where – hopefully – it has a nice row of unmoved pawns to protect it from a frontal assault.

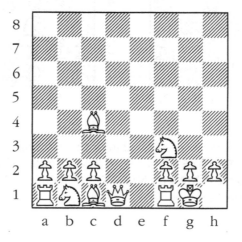

The diagram shows a very safe-looking white king hiding behind the defensive wall of pawns. Note also that by castling White has very much brought his king's rook into the game; this piece will certainly enjoy aiming down one of the open files in the centre.

The Weak King in the Centre

If the centre is open or, perhaps more precisely, if the e-file is completely open, leaving your king in the centre is often hazardous, especially if your opponent has castled and his rook is ready to give check.

The following example is typical: Black has a chance to escape to relative safety via castling but doesn't take it and pays the ultimate price.

1 e4 e5 2 Nf3 Nc6 3 Bc4

This opening is called the Giuoco Piano (it's also known as the Italian Game), and it's very popular amongst junior players – often it's the first opening they really learn.

3...Bc5 4 c3 Nf6 5 d4 exd4 6 cxd4 Bb4+ 7 Nc3

I'm not going into any detail here over the opening moves because we'll study this line in Chapter 6. I will just mention here though that Black should probably grab the pawn on offer with 7...Nxe4!.

7...d5 8 exd5 Nxd5 9 0-0 Bxc3 10 bxc3

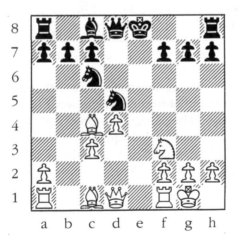

So far it's been pretty normal stuff, with both sides developing sensibly. Black now has a really good opportunity to castle and bring his king into safety. Instead he decides to delay this for just one move, preferring to retreat the knight to attack the bishop on c4.

10...Nb6?

The bishop is attacked so it has to retreat, right?

11 Re1+!

Wrong!

11...Kf8

In an ideal world Black would have preferred to have blocked the check, since moving the king forfeits castling rights. Unfortunately there was no suitable block available: 11...Ne7 allows White to exploit the pin with 12 Ba3!, and following 12...Nxc4 13 Rxe7+ Black is forced to give up his queen as 13...Kf8 allows a devastating discovered check with 14 Rd7+. The move 11...Be6 is not quite as disastrous, but following 12 Bxe6 fxe6 13 Rxe6+ White has an extra pawn and Black's king is no safer than it was before.

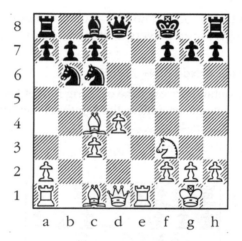

The fact that Black has lost his castling rights means that even after the mundane 12 Bb3, moving the bishop out of trouble, White would already be well on top. It's not that the black king would be particularly poorly placed (after all, one move to g8 would see it reach its normal castled square), it's just that it would be very difficult for Black to get his h8-rook into play with the king blocking it (those of you who were about to suggest ...h5 and ...Rh6, lose ten points and read Chapter 2 again).

It just so happens here that White has something much more destructive...

12 Bxf7!! Kxf7

Of course Black wasn't forced to capture the bishop, but if he doesn't White has just ripped away a vital defensive pawn at no cost.

13 Ng5+!

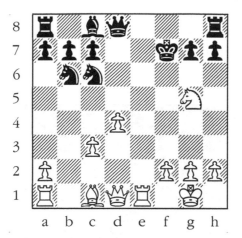

13...Kg8

It soon becomes apparent that wherever the king goes, it cannot avoid a barrage of checks. The line 13...Kf8 14 Ba3+ Kg8 15 Qb3+ is very similar to the main text, while 13...Kf6 14 Qf3+ Kg6 15 Qf7+! Kh6 gives White the opportunity to play a crushing discovered check with 16 Ne6. The only other defensive try for Black is 13...Kg6 but this loses to 14 Qd3+! Kh5 (or 14...Bf5 15 Re6+! when Black has to give up his queen with 15...Qf6 or else allow complete carnage with 15...Kh5 16 Qxf5) 15 Re6!!

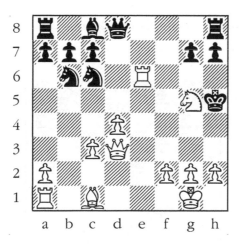

(threatening mate in one with Qh3, so Black is forced to accept the sacrifice) 15...Bxe6 16 Nxe6 Qf6 17 Nxg7+! Qxg7 18 Qf5+ Kh4 19 Qh3 and finally it's checkmate.

There were a few long and tricky variations in the previous paragraph. Don't worry too much if some of it was difficult to follow. The main point is to realize that Black's king is in great danger when devoid of cover and exposed to powerful enemy pieces. And of course all of this could have easily been avoided had Black played the sensible 10...0-0.

14 Qb3+ Nd5

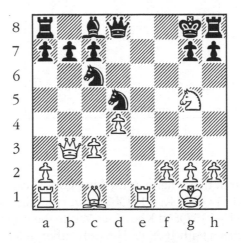

14...Qd5 would have allowed mate in one with 15 Re8. Just for a moment it looks as if Black has everything covered after 14...Nd5, but White has up his sleeve a wicked queen sacrifice.

15 Qxd5+!!

Deflecting the black queen from its back rank duties.

15...Qxd5 16 Re8 mate!

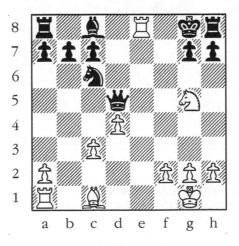

A very nice checkmate to finish off a powerful demonstration of what can happen to a king if it finds itself in the firing line.

Points to Remember

1) Failure to castle out of trouble is one of the main reasons behind early losses.

2) A check trumps any other threat! In the previous example Black may have thought that White would be forced to retreat the bishop on move eleven, but this illusion was shattered by 11 Re1+!.

Fool's Mate

The quickest possible checkmate arises after only two moves and is known as fool's mate. Unlike scholar's mate (see page 19), one has to be more than just careless to allow it. In fact, it requires an exact sequence of accommodating play by the loser: it is what those in the problem solving world would term a 'helpmate' – one player helps the other to deliver checkmate.

1 f3?

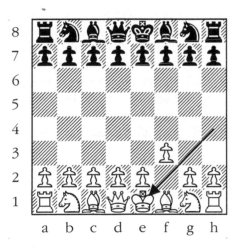

This is probably White's worst possible choice as an opening move; certainly it is in terms of king safety. For no good reason at all, White has exposed his king on the newly opened h4-e1 diagonal (more about moving the f-pawn like this a bit later).

1...e5

A good move, lining up ...Qh4!

2 g4??

The 'star move' that conveniently prevents White from blocking the queen check. This move is so accommodating that it's the equivalent of a paid-off boxer taking a fall in the first round.

2...Qh4 mate!

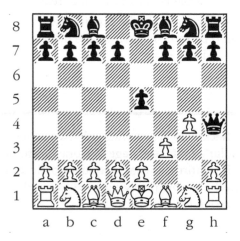

There it is! Unfortunately I have never had the pleasure of seeing this checkmate occur in real life, and I must admit I did have a cheeky look at a chess database of over 3,000,000 games, but no luck there either. Still, every chess player worth his salt needs to know fool's mate, if nothing else to keep his head above water when the conversation turns to quick checkmates. Many newcomers get it confused with the infinitely more frequent scholar's mate. Both emphasize the problem with the f-pawn: scholar's mate demonstrates the vulnerability of the f-pawn on its original square, while fool's mate illustrates a problem with moving the f-pawn.

Trouble with the f-pawn

By now you must be getting used to the idea that the f-pawn needs to be handled with great care in the opening. Here's another brief example to underline the problems.

1 e4 e5 2 Nf3

We've already come across this sequence quite a few times.

2...f6?

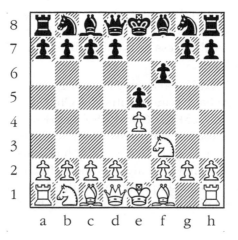

This way of defending the e5-pawn is not that uncommon in games between new-comers, but it should be avoided at all costs! There are three very good reasons why 2...f6 is such a poor move:

1) It neither develops a piece nor opens a line for a piece to be developed.

2) It deprives the king's knight of its favourite developing post: the f6-square.

3) Most significantly, it weakens the black king terribly, both along the h5-e8 diagonal and the a2-g8 diagonal.

3 Bc4!

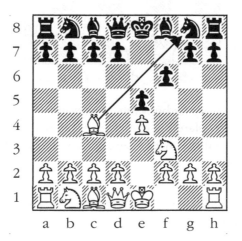

3 Bc4 isn't the only good move for White here, but it does illustrate more than anything else one of the major problems behind Black's previous move. In 1 e4 e5

openings, the bishop is normally well placed on c4, but with the f-pawn moved its scope along the a2-g8 diagonal has increased further: it now attacks the g8-square. A crucial consequence of this is that Black won't be able to legally castle kingside (you can't castle into check!) unless he is able to block this diagonal, and this is more easily said than done.

That said, the capture 3 Nxe5! is also very tempting, since following the obvious recapture 3...fxe5? White has a winning attack: 4 Qh5+! Ke7 (or 4...g6 5 Qxe5+, forking king and rook) 5 Qxe5+ Kf7 6 Bc4+ d5 7 Bxd5+ Kg6 8 h4! (threatening h5+) 8...h5 9 Bxb7! (deflecting the bishop) 9...Bxb7 (or else the rook in the corner gets captured) 10 Qf5+ Kh6 11 d4+ g5 12 Bxg5+ and White wins. 3...Qe7! is more resilient, when the tempting 4 Qh5+ actually falls short after 4...g6 5 Nxg6 Qxe4+! and 6...Qxg6. Instead White should simply retreat with 4 Nf3, and following 4...Qxe4+ 5 Be2 White will increase his development advantage by gaining time on the black queen.

3...Nc6 4 Nh4!?

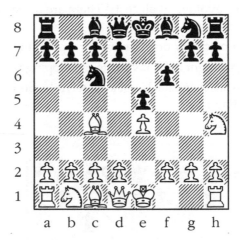

You can see what White is up to: he wants to exploit the weakness of 2...f6 immediately by playing 5 Qh5+, planning to answer 5...g6 with 6 Nxg6! fxg6 7 Qxh8. Black should prevent this threat with 4...g6, but what happens if he tries to get rid of that annoying knight?

4...g5??

Going into a kind of fool's mate mode! White is only happy to oblige.

5 Qh5+ Ke7 6 Nf5 mate!

Another horrible disaster involving the f-pawn. I hope the message is getting through!

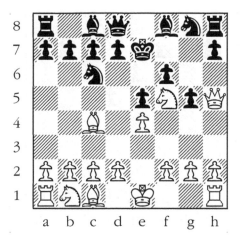

Attacking f7

In 1 e4 e5 openings the f-pawn in its original position (f7 for Black; f2 for White) is sometimes referred to as the Achilles heel of a player's position, and this is easy to explain why. Firstly, it's easy to attack and, secondly, it's the only pawn which lacks protection by a piece other than the king.

We've already seen in Chapter 1 a direct attempt to exploit the weakness via scholar's mate. There are, however, numerous more subtle and, in the final analysis, more dangerous ways of attacking this pawn (or the square if the pawn moves). The following example shows an attacking technique that is very commonly seen in games between improving players.

1 e4 e5 2 Nf3 d6

This is known as Philidor's Defence. If Black is going to defend e5 with a pawn, 2...d6 is a much better choice than 2...f6. Black opens a route of development for the light-squared bishop, although on the minus side the f8-bishop is blocked and thus has fewer options.

3 Bc4 Nc6 4 Nc3

Typical, sensible development so far.

Question: Black wishes to develop his kingside minor pieces and castle. Should he develop his bishop first, his knight first, or does it make no difference.

Answer: Those of you who employed the 'knights before bishops' guideline will be disappointed: the move order does make a difference and Black should play 4...Be7!.

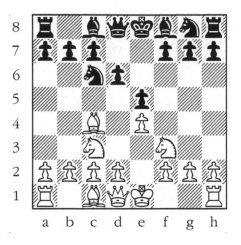

Actually, going back to the previous paragraph, this is a good illustration of why guidelines should be treated as such, not as hard and fast rules. Firstly, 4...Nf6 fails for tactical reasons as we shall see; secondly, the bishop really only has one possible developing square (e7), and given that 'knights before bishops' is merely an extension of 'only develop a piece once you are sure you know the best place for it', this argument falls down here.

Let's get back to 4...Nf6 and why Black should avoid playing it here.

4...Nf6? 5 Ng5!

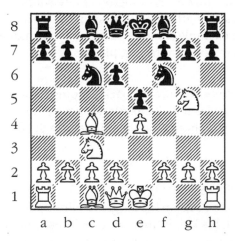

Suddenly the f7-pawn is attacked twice and Black has no good way to defend it (I'll leave you to work out why defending it with the queen doesn't deal with the threat). Worse still, not only is White threatening to take a pawn, he's also aiming for some destruction in the process: Bxf7+ will force the black king to move, eliminating Black's castling rights; Nxf7, forking queen and rook and thus winning material, is even more of a worry. Black can block the attack along the a2-g8 diagonal in two ways, but neither is satisfactory: both 5...Be6 6 Nxe6 fxe6 7 Bxe6 and 5...d5 6 exd5 leave Black a pawn down.

Going back to the position after White's fourth move, Black could have avoided the strife with his f7-pawn with...

4...Be7!

Now Ng5 is prevented for the moment – the g5-square is covered – and so White must get on with development. After, say...

5 0-0

...only now does Black play...

5...Nf6

It's true that White can then plough ahead with

6 Ng5?!

...but now Black is ready to kill two birds with one stone by playing

6...0-0!

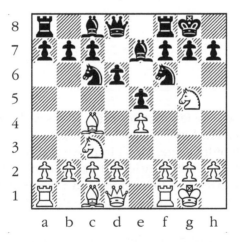

By castling Black has provided crucial support to the f7-pawn and brought his king into relative safety at the same time.

Question: From the diagrammed position above, who if anyone gains from the exchange of material after 7 Nxf7 Rxf7 8 Bxf7+ Kxf7?

Answer: Black gains from the trade.

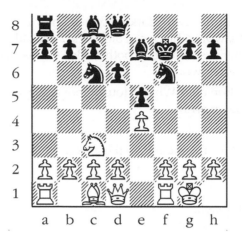

This last Q & A brings up an interesting point because I've witnessed this type of exchange time and time again in junior chess. Let's just remind ourselves of the traditionally accepted value of the chess pieces:

Queen: 9 points
Rook: 5 points
Bishop: 3 points
Knight: 3 points
Pawn: 1 point

So in a traditional sense it's a fair exchange (six points each). However, we've already talked about rooks disliking the opening stages of the game, and I could add to this by saying that they often don't improve that much going into the early middlegame phase. It's generally considered that, everything else being equal, two minor pieces are worth more than a rook and a pawn in the middlegame. Only in the endgame, where the rooks appreciate the wide open spaces, is real parity restored.

Perhaps one of the things that entices inexperienced players into entering this trade is the fact that on the surface Black's king looks a bit vulnerable on f7. With more experience, however, players soon realize that this is just an illusion. In reality the king is quite safe where it is, and it's only a hop away from g8. To be vulnerable there needs to be pieces that can attack the king, and it has to be remembered here that White has just given up two of his most active pieces: the bishop on c4 and the knight on g5.

Exercises

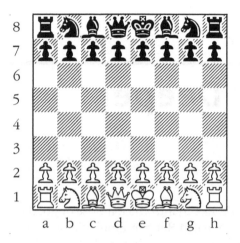

1) Imagine that White has been allowed four moves without reply. Can you suggest a sensible sequence that would end up with White's king castled?

2) Consider the position after **1 e4 e5 2 Bc4 Nf6 3 d3 Nc6 4 Nc3 Bc5** and now **5 Nge2**.

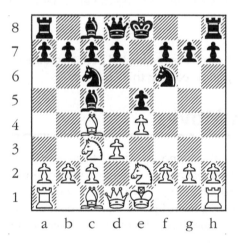

a) Why is White's previous move a big mistake?

b) Why can't 5 Nf3 be punished in the same way?

Chapter Four

Delving Deeper

To begin this chapter, I'd like to introduce a dose of good old-fashioned common sense. When I recently revisited Reuben Fine's classic *The Ideas behind Chess Openings* (still essential reading for more advanced players) I was struck by reading that there are two questions you should ask yourself for each move you are about to play. These are:

1) How does this move affect the centre?

2) How does this move fit in with the development of my other pieces and pawns?

Sometimes the simplest advice is the best! These two questions are certainly worth keeping in mind throughout reading this chapter.

Luxury Pawn Moves

One of the things I've spotted amongst those fairly new to the game is the tendency to play unnecessary pawn moves early in the opening. In many respects these could be described as luxury pawn moves: they are not necessarily weakening; they might even have a useful point (see the next paragraph); however, crucially they lose valuable time in the development race, and this is often the most critical factor of the position.

The 'reasoning' behind such a pawn move is normally to prevent the possibility of an enemy piece entering into home territory. If time were not a factor this would be all well and good, but of course this is usually not the case. The problem is that often the fear of the intrusion proves to be unfounded, and it turns out that the tempo could have been more purposefully used elsewhere (development).

Of course the danger of losing time with redundant pawn moves cannot be underestimated. I make no apologies for using the following famous example to show how one could get punished to the full.

1 e4 e5 2 Nf3 d6

We came across Philidor's Defence on page 55. It's true that 2...d6 is not quite as active as 2...Nc6 (it means the dark-squared bishop will probably have to make do with the passive e7-square), but it's not a bad move all the same. For one thing, the bishop on c8 is now ready to be developed.

3 Bc4 Bg4 4 Nc3

So far both sides have developed sensibly (the development score is 4-3 in White's favour with Black to move). It's certainly not obvious, but White actually has a threat here...

4...h6?

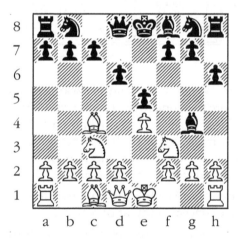

Definitely an unnecessary pawn move! Its reasoning could be described as follows: Black is worried about the possibility in the future of Ng5, attacking f7, so decides to rule out it out forever. This decision making, however, could be described as both lazy and short-sighted. Firstly, White is a long way from playing this move: g5 is covered by the black queen and White's knight is pinned to the queen (although see White's next move!). Secondly, we have already seen from page 57 that there's another way to deal with the Ng5 idea in the form of preparing to castle.

Before looking at alternatives, let's see how Black's failure to develop leads to a dramatic denouement.

5 Nxe5!!

It turns out it was another knight move that Black should have been worrying about! Now if Black captures the knight with 5...dxe5 White replies with 6 Qxg4 when he has won a pawn. But isn't there a queen en prise here?

5...Bxd1 6 Bxf7+! Ke7

The only legal move.

7 Nd5 mate!

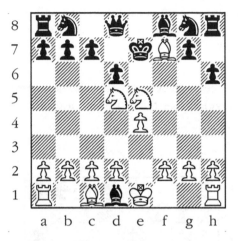

A very pretty checkmate; White's bishop and two knights combine beautifully. This mate, which has more than one form, (White could have played the same way against the superfluous 4...a6) is actually known as Legall's mate, named after the 18th century French player Legall de Kermeur. Note that every possible escape square for the king is covered once and only once by a white piece. Students of chess puzzles would call this a 'pure mate'.

Going back to the position after White's fourth move, it's now clear to us that White has a very cleverly concealed threat of 5 Nxe5!.

Question: Can Black deal with this threat by playing a natural developing move?

Answer: Yes! And there is more than one way.

Firstly, let's try the move...

4...Nc6!

(see following diagram)

Now, if White tries the same trick with...

5 Nxe5??

...hoping for Legall's mate after 5...Bxd1?? 6 Bxf7+ Ke7 7 Nd5, Black can spoil the party by refusing the offer of the queen and instead play the cold-blooded...

5...Nxe5!

...leaving him a knight for a pawn to the good in the material stakes. Note that the crucial difference to the line 4...h6? 5 Nxe5! dxe5 is that here the bishop on g4 is protected by the knight on e5, thus making it invulnerable to the white queen.

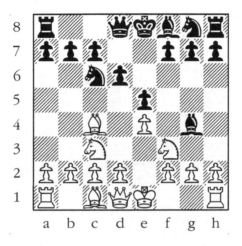

Secondly, let's go for another developing move with...

4...Nf6!

What happens now if White goes for the flashy mate? Let's see.

5 Nxe5?? Bxd1! 6 Bxf7+ Ke7

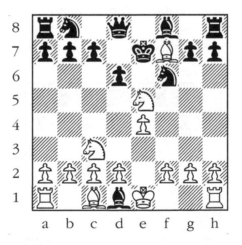

And now the trick doesn't work as Black has the d5-square covered (7 Nd5+ is met simply by 7...Nxd5) and so White is a queen down. Note that there was a second refutation to 5 Nxe5?? in the shape of 5...dxe5, when again the bishop is protected on g4.

So Black has at least two perfectly good developing moves to deal with the threat after 4 Nc3 (in fact there are more; I'll leave you to work out what they are).

To be fair, it's unusual to be punished so brutally when playing a luxury pawn move, but even so it's always worth checking whether there is a more economic way out before settling for such a pawn move. Take the following example:

1 d4 c6 2 e4 d5 3 exd5 cxd5 4 Nc3 Nc6 5 Bf4

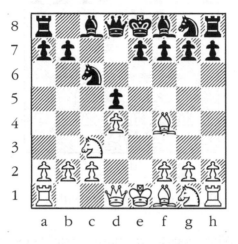

In this example Black is rightly concerned about the possibility of Nb5-c7+, forking the king and rook.

Question: 5...a6 would eliminate this problem, but can you seen a more economic way for Black to deal with White's idea?

Answer: Black can play 5...Bf5!. Now Black is ready to meet 6 Nb5 with 6...Rc8!,

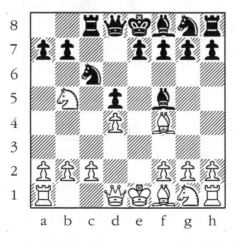

covering the c7-square and thus preventing Nc7+ (this would then lose a bishop and knight for a rook). Black is now ready to kick the knight back to c3 with ...a7-a6. The difference between 5...Bf5 and 5...a6 is that in the latter Black deals with White's threat with a good, solid developing move.

I don't want to give the impression that this type of preventative move (...a6, ...h6) is always superfluous. Sometimes a move like this is the only good way forward:
1 e4 e6 2 d4 d5 3 Nc3 dxe4 4 Nxe4 Nd7 5 Nf3 Ngf6 6 Nxf6+ Nxf6 7 c3 c5

7...c5 nibbles away at White's d4-pawn, so it's a very logical part of battling for central control. On the other hand, it does mean that Black has to watch out for checks on the a4-e8 diagonal as they can no longer be blocked by the simple ...c7-c6. At the moment 8 Bb5+ or 8 Qa4+ can be safely answered by 8...Bd7, but...

8 Ne5!

Aggressive play! White's knight is very actively placed on e5 and with it covering the d7-square, the check on the diagonal suddenly carries more bite. Let's see what can happen if Black carries on with development and allows the check.

8...Bd6?! 9 Bb5+!

Now unless Black moves his king, thus forfeiting castling rights, he has to make a block on d7. However, neither is totally satisfactory.

9...Nd7

9...Bd7 10 Nxd7! Nxd7 11 dxc5! Bxc5 leaves Black in a perilous position due to the pin on the knight. One nice continuation is 12 Qh5!? (threatening the pinned bishop; 12...0-0 loses a piece to 13 Bxd7 Qxd7 14 Qxc5) 12...Be7 and now quick as a flash *Fritz* comes out with 13 Bh6!! gxh6 14 Rd1!, exploiting the pin on the knight to the full. White will follow up with Rxd7 when Black is in big trouble.

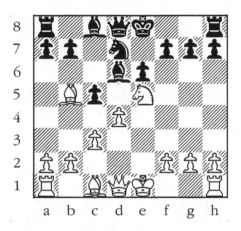

10 Qg4!

White continues in energetic fashion by attacking the g7-pawn. This position actually occurred in one of Garry Kasparov's games (White against Ruslan Ponomariov at Linares 2002). Here Ponomariov felt obliged to give up his castling rights by playing 10...Kf8. Obviously this was not an ideal scenario for the then FIDE Champion, but alternatives fall short. In particular, the desirable 10...0-0? loses material after 11 Bxd7 Bxd7 12 Bh6!, when Black's best bet is to give up an exchange with 12...g6. Another way to deal with the threat to the g-pawn is with 10...g6, but then White can still prevent Black from castling queenside by playing 11 Bh6!.

Let's go back to the position after 8 Ne5. After the Kasparov-Ponomariov encounter, grandmasters came to the conclusion that a 'preventative' pawn move was the best course of action:

8...a6!

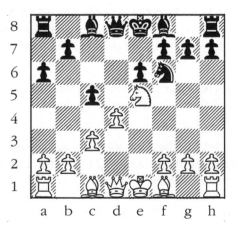

Crucially the move Bb5 has been ruled out of the equation, and grandmaster analysis has shown that Black doesn't suffer unduly by playing a non-developing move.

Luxury pawn moves are often more affordable once development is at a later stage, as seen in the next example.

1 e4 e5 2 Nf3 Nc6 3 Bb5 a6 4 Ba4 Nf6 5 d3 b5 6 Bb3 Bc5 7 0-0 d6 8 c3 0-0

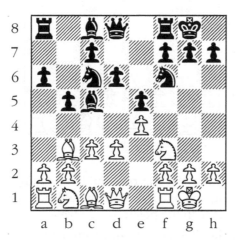

Here both sides have developed well. White has numerous options here, including developing the dark-squared bishop (9 Bg5 and 9 Be3, offering a trade, come to mind). There is, however, also something to be said for 9 h3, which eliminates all future possibilities of ...Bg4 and ...Ng4. And against 9 h3 there's an argument for Black to follow suit with 9...h6, preventing both Ng5 and Bg5 (we'll discuss this Bg5/...Bg4 pin in more detail a bit later.

Point to Remember

Ask yourself some questions before playing 'preventative' pawn moves in the opening. Is there really time to play the move? Could you survive without it? Does it create further weaknesses?

Moving a Piece Twice

'Don't move the same piece twice in the opening!' is a guideline that newcomers are likely to hear from chess teachers and more experienced players. The logical idea behind this is that you should concentrate on developing the rest of your pieces first before embarking on a solitary mission with just one of them. Of course over-emphasis on this guideline can lead (and, as I've seen, has led) to confusion amongst inexperienced players. Take the following snippet:

1 Nf3 e5?

Black has left a vital central pawn en prise, but those taking 'don't move the same piece twice in the opening' too much to heart would possibly have serious doubts about playing the best move in the position – 2 Nxe5!.

Adding a few words makes it a more accurate guideline: 'Don't move the same piece twice in the opening without good reason.'

Sometimes it's fairly obvious that a second move with the same piece leads nowhere, for example:

1 d4 Nf6 2 Nf3 g6 3 c4 Bg7 4 Nc3 0-0 5 e3 d6 6 Nb5?

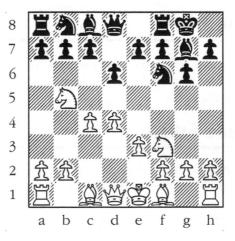

It should be easy to recognize that White is nowhere near in a position to attack deep into Black's queenside and the knight advance cannot be supported. The knight on b5 offers no threat and Black could either totally ignore it or attack it with...

6...a6

Now 7 Nc3 is surely White's best retreat, which only underlines the futility of White's sixth move: it simply loses valuable time.

If every example was as clear-cut as the previous one, this would be an easy guideline to follow. However, it becomes more complicated when the player in question is enticed into creating a solid threat. Let's go back to an idea we looked at earlier: the possibility of an early attack on the f7-pawn.

1 e4 e5 2 Nf3 Nc6 3 Bc4 Bc5 4 d3 Nf6 5 0-0 d6 6 Ng5?!

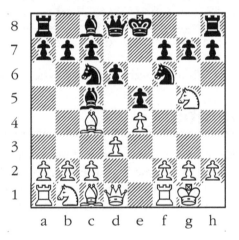

Inexperienced players often find the possibility of playing Nf3-g5 in such a position too difficult to resist. Their reasoning goes something like:

1) Black might not spot the threat!
2) Okay he might, but it's worth a gamble!

The problem is that after the likely event of Black finding the move...

6...0-0!

...there is no good follow-up for White to continue the attack (7 Qh5, attacking f7 again, would be nice but it leaves the queen en prise). We've already seen that the trade on f7 with 7 Nxf7 Rxf7 8 Bxf7+ Kxf7 favours Black more than White, but what happens if White carries on developing?

7 Nc3 h6! 8 Nf3

Quite rightly White dismisses 8 Nh3?.

8...Bg4

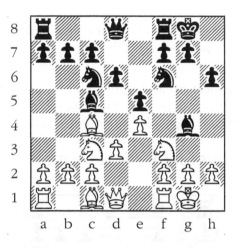

Due to the meandering of White's knight, it's Black who is ahead on development!

Point to Remember

It's very easy to be seduced into making a second move with a piece in order to create a threat, but you have to assume that direct threats will be spotted by your opponent. In this case you have to ask yourself what the consequences are. Does your position really improve? Is your piece better placed than before? Will it be quickly pushed back?

Grabbing Pawns

Chess is a very materialistic game – the player with the most pieces is the one who normally ends up winning – so you should always be on the lookout for any possibilities to capture material. Before you decide to grab a pawn (it's less likely that your opponent will leave a piece en prise) there are one or two (or three) questions that are worth asking:

1) Does this allow a trick?
2) Will this expose my king?
3) Will I fall behind on development?

Obviously if the answer to '1' is 'yes' then assume your opponent has seen the trick and simply ignore the pawn. If the answer to either '2' or '3' is yes then you have to use your judgement. How vital is that pawn in the long run? Is winning that pawn worth all the hassle you're going to get?

Let's have a look at a possible continuation in the Ruy Lopez.

1 e4 e5 2 Nf3 Nc6 3 Bb5 a6 4 Ba4 b5 5 Bb3 Nf6 6 0-0

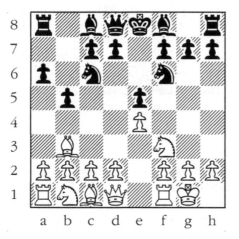

On White's last move there were ways to defend the threatened e4-pawn (6 d3, 6 Nc3 and 6 Qe2 come to mind), but instead he chose to ignore it and castled instead. The question is should Black grab the pawn on e4?

Let's look at the three questions above. We'll ignore the first one for the moment because to determine whether it's a trick or not needs some analysis. So, will taking the pawn on e4 expose Black's king? It's certainly a possibility because one of the two pawns on the e-file is removed. It only takes the removal of the e5-pawn and the e-file will be totally open and the king will be vulnerable to a check (Re1 or Qe2). Secondly, will Black fall behind in development? Here the answer is yes because White can gain time attacking the knight on e4.

Against all this Black has to weigh up the value of winning a pawn. This isn't any old pawn; it's a crucial central pawn. If Black were able to get away with taking it then it would be a prize scalp.

Working on general principles is obviously useful, but at the end of the day some analysis is required for Black to make a decision.

6...Nxe4 7 Re1!

A typical reaction and much stronger than 7 d3. Now if the knight moves out of the way, the e5-pawn will be en prise.

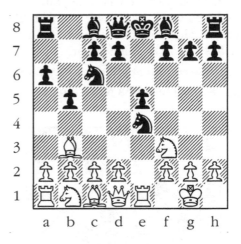

7...d5!

Supporting the knight and allowing the c8-bishop to develop. I believe this is stronger than immediately retreating the knight. For example, 7...Nc5 can be met by 8 Bd5! when threats include Nxe5 and d2-d4. The most obvious retreat is 7...Nf6, and now 8 Nxe5 Nxe5 9 Rxe5+ Be7 10 Qe2 is slightly awkward for Black because the attack on the e7-bishop means that he can't castle for the moment. As well as 9 Rxe5+, White can also exploit the pin on the e-file with 9 d4!, which looks even stronger as White ends up with a powerful pawn on e5: for example, 9...Be7? 10 dxe5 Ng8 (there's nothing else!) 11 Qd5 threatening mate on f7 and the rook on h8; or 8...Bb7 10 dxe5 Ne4 11 Qf3!...

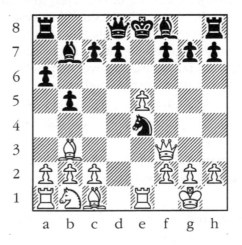

...and again White wins material, this time due to the double attack on f7 and e4

(note that 11...Nd6 loses to 12 exd6 – check!).

8 d3

By attacking the knight with the pawn, White ensures that the knight must retreat...

8...Nf6

...and now White can win his pawn back.

9 Nxe5 Nxe5 10 Rxe5+

With the knight being pinned to the king, White can also consider not recapturing at once, instead playing 10 d4!? with the intention of capturing with the pawn. This is quite a threat since it would attack the knight and leave Black's d-pawn en prise. However, with some careful play Black can ensure a reasonable position with 10...Be6 (defending d5) 11 dxe5 Ne4!.

10...Be6!

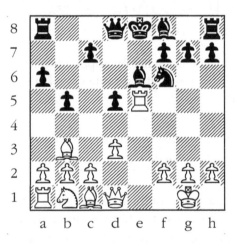

White has managed to give a check on the e-file, but Black's last move has securely blocked the file. White can't really do much to prevent Black following up with ...Bd6 and ...0-0, after which Black's problems disappear and he has reached an equal position.

So grabbing on e4 looks perfectly playable after some initial analysis, although it's true that Black has to tread carefully for one or two moves. Going back to question '1', 'does this allow a trick?', the answer is 'yes', but only one that regains the pawn with no advantage so this is not enough of a deterrent for Black.

On the other hand, if one is trying to be thorough, it's not enough to look only at 7 Re1: the similar move 7 Qe2 comes into consideration too, while there's no rule that says that White must try to regain his pawn immediately.

Question: Can you suggest a way for White to both further his development and blow open the centre?

Answer: White can play **7 d4!**.

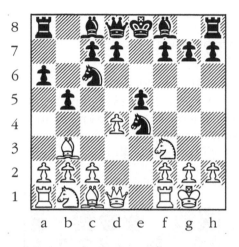

The attraction of this move is immediately apparent: White opens the way for his c1-bishop and attacks the e5-pawn at the same time. Let's see what happens if Black goes 'pawn happy'.

7...exd4?!

Question: Can you spot an obvious flaw with 7...Nxd4?

Answer: White can play 8 Nxd4 exd4 9 Bd5!, forking the rook and knight.

8 Re1! d5!

Instead 8...f5? runs into the 'curse of the f-pawn'. After 9 Ng5! White threatens both Nf7, forking queen and rook, and f2-f3, winning the pinned knight.

After 8...d5 Black could be forgiven for thinking that he was out of the woods, as obvious attempts by White do not amount to much. Black is okay after 9 Nxd4 Nxd4 10 Qxd4 Be6! (and especially after 11 f3?? Bc5!), while 9 Nbd2 Be7 10 Nxe4 dxe4 11 Rxe4 0-0 also solves Black's problems. However, there's another possibility...

9 Nc3!!

(see following diagram)

Amazingly this works! Once Black has realized that there's only one legal way to capture the knight, he has to face up to the problems surrounding e4 and d5.

9...dxc3

9...Be6 is possible, but following 10 Nxe4 dxe4 11 Rxe4 Black still has major problems on the open e-file (11...Qd7 12 Ng5 is one example). Relatively best is 11...Be7, and after 12 Bxe6 fxe6 13 Nxd4 0-0 it's true that Black has managed to castle. White does, however, keep an advantage after 14 Qg4 Nxd4 15 Rxd4, when the material balance has been restored and Black has a weak isolated pawn on e6. This position actually occurred in one of Bobby Fischer's games (he was White versus Trifunovic, Bled 1961).

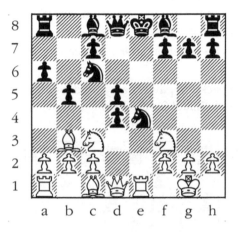

10 Bxd5

The point behind White's previous move: d5 drops and White regains the temporarily sacrificed piece because both knights are en prise.

10...Bb7 11 Bxe4 Be7

Black has no time to exchange queens, as 11...Qxd1?? fails to the zwischenzug 12 Bxc6+! Kd8 13 Rxd1+, leaving White a piece ahead.

12 Qe2!

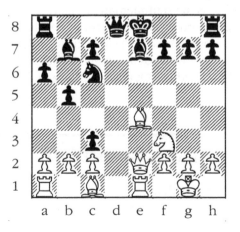

A very important move; White doesn't allow the exchange of queens, which would seriously diminish his attacking chances. Just as importantly, White prevents Black from castling, as 12...0-0? would lose the bishop on e7 after 13 Bxc6! Bxc6 14 Qxe7. So Black has a very difficult times ahead, and one line illustrating his problems is 12...Qd6 13 Bxc6+ Bxc6 14 Bg5! f6 15 Rad1! Qc5 16 b4! Qxb4 17 Qe6! Bxf3 18 Rd7 Be4 19 a3! (and not 19 Rxe4? which allows Black to escape with 19...Qb1+ 20 Re1 Qxe1+ 21 Qxe1 Kxd7) 19...Qxa3 20 Bc1! Qb4 21 Rxe4 Qxe4 22 Rxe7+ and it's mate next move. A long variation, but it's quite easy to see that Black is suffering in many ways here.

Question: Going back to the position after 7 d4!, can you suggest a good way for Black to continue?

Answer: Black can give back the pawn, carry on developing and consolidate his position in the centre with **7...d5! 8 dxe5 Be6!**.

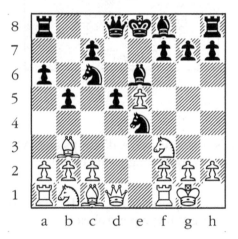

Contrast this position with the one after 7...exd4. Here the e-file is blocked by three pieces – Black's king is in no immediate danger. Also, Black's knight on e4 is well supported by the pawn on d5, which in turn is protected by the bishop and queen. All in all, Black's position is satisfactory. Indeed this position has been reached literally thousands of times at all levels of chess (albeit via a slightly different move order) and is called the Open Variation of the Ruy Lopez.

Gaining Time

It's already been mentioned how useful it is to be able to develop and create a threat at the same time, thus gaining valuable time in the development race. Likewise, it's good to be able to defend against a threat with a developing move. Here I'd like to look at two more openings where these ideas are prominent:

1 e4 e5 2 Nf3 Nc6 3 d4

White decides to open the centre immediately. This is known as the Scotch Game.

3...exd4 4 Nxd4

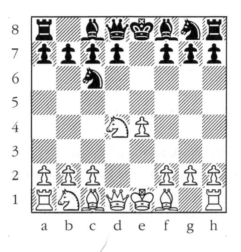

I gave this position to some young chess students who had very little knowledge of opening theory and certainly no knowledge of the Scotch Game. I asked them to look for two or three moves for Black and for each of these, two or three replies for White and so on, keeping in mind the idea of gaining time with threats and answering threats with a developing move. The results were pleasing: they ended up recreating modern opening theory! Here's a summary of some of the lines suggested:

A) 4...Bc5!

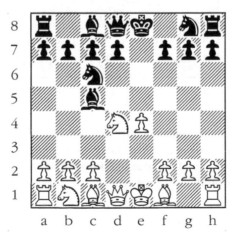

This was the favourite choice amongst the students, and it just so happens to be the most popular choice in modern tournament chess! The benefits of this move are obvious: Black develops a kingside piece and gains time by attacking the d4-knight.

5 Be3!

Not only defending the threat with a developing move, but also creating a threat too.

Question: What is White threatening?

Answer: 6 Nxc6, uncovering an attack on the bishop, followed by 7 Bxc5.

Here are some of the other good suggestions:

1) 5 Nf5 gains time by attacking the g7-pawn.

2) 5 Nb3 turns the tables; now it's the knight that is attacking the bishop.

3) 5 Nxc6 is also a time-gaining move. Rather than simply retreating the knight, White trades on c6 when Black is forced to spend his move on a simple recapture.

5...Qf6!

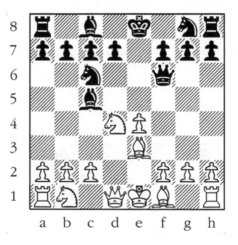

An excellent move, though it requires a touch of calculation. Black is able to take measures against White's threat and also keep up the pressure on the d4-knight. What more could you ask? It's true that Black must be careful not to expose the queen, but in this position it's not particularly vulnerable on f6.

5...Bb6 is another, less economical, way of addressing the threat. One or two students suggested protecting the bishop with the developing 5...d6?, but were rightly put off after seeing the continuation 6 Nxc6! bxc6 7 Bxc5 dxc5: Black's tripled c-pawns are not a happy sight!

After 5...Qf6 White must do something about the attack on d4 again:

1) 6 Nxc6 Bxe3! is the point behind 5...Qf6: after 7 fxe3 (forced because mate was threatened on f2) Black can recapture on c6.

2) 6 c3 is a solid way of defending d4 and is White's most common choice in tournament play.

3) Given that the brief was to look for moves that gained time with threats, 6 Nb5!? is a logical choice. Following 6...Bxe3 7 fxe3 Black has to expend time defending against the threat of Nxc7+. The flipside, of course, is that White is left with ghastly doubled, isolated pawns (more about this in Chapter 5).

B) 4...Nf6!

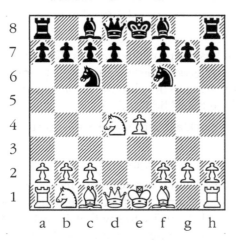

Another move that was suggested by quite a few students. Again Black develops with a threat; this time it's the e4-pawn that's the target.

5 Nc3

Unfortunately for White the natural 5 Bd3?? leaves the knight hanging on d4. That point led to the suggestion of 5 Nxc6 bxc6 and only then 6 Bd3, or 6 e5 gaining time by attacking the knight.

5...Bb4!

Consistent play from Black: by pinning the c3-knight, the e4-pawn is again attacked and Black is already prepared for castling kingside.

Question: If Black turned his attention back to the d4-knight with 5...Bc5, could you name three good ways to deal with the threat?

Answer: 6 Nb3 (attacking the bishop), 6 Be3 (threatening to win a piece with Nxc6), and 6 Nxc6 (forcing Black to recapture). All three moves gain time.

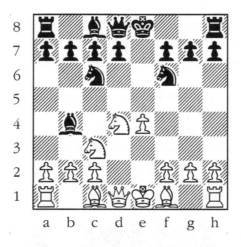

After 5...Bb4, White still has the problem that 6 Bd3?? leaves the d4-knight en prise. The logical moves suggested here were: 6 Bg5, pinning the f6-knight to the black queen; 6 Qd3, preparing to develop the c1-bishop and castle queenside; and 6 Nxc6 bxc6 followed by either 7 Bd3 or 7 e5.

Question: Going back to Black's fourth move, can you suggest any other options that create a threat?

Answer: 4...Bb4+, 4...Qf6, 4...Qh4, 4...Qe7 and 4...d5.

It's difficult to go into the pros and cons of these moves without delving too much into the theory of the Scotch Game, and that certainly isn't the idea of this book. I'll leave you to decide on this; suffice to say that 4...Bb4+ and 4...Qf6 are very reasonable moves, 4...Qh4 is interesting but risky, and 4...Qe7 and 4...d5 are both considered dubious.

The Queen: Exposed or Not?

In Chapter 2 we talked just a little bit about queen handling in the opening, but here I'd like to expand on this by taking a look at two positions which look quite similar but contain subtle differences.

The first position arises after the moves...

1 e4 e5 2 d4 exd4 3 Qxd4

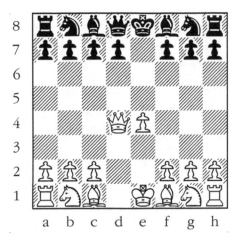

This opening is known as the Centre Game, but it's not very popular at any level of chess for reasons we are about to discover.

Question: Can you spot a good move for Black?

Answer: 4...Nc6!.

After reading the previous section, I hope you got this! 4...Nc6 is clearly Black's best move: it develops a piece and gains time because White's queen is forced to move again.

4 Qe3

Theory considers this to be the main move, although there's an argument for moving the queen to the a4-square; at least there it's less likely to come under further attack. After 4 Qe3 White can still claim to be ahead in the development race (2-1) and plans to play Nc3, Bd2 and 0-0-0.

4...Nf6!

Meanwhile, Black's ideas include developing rapidly on the kingside and possibly ganging up on the e4-pawn.

5 Nc3

When Black plays ...Nf6 he always has to take into account the advance e4-e5, but following 5 e5 Black can again take advantage of White's exposed queen with 5...Ng4 6 Qe4...

(see following diagram)

...and now Black has two enticing possibilities:

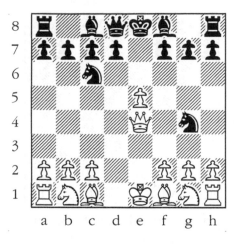

1) 6...Ngxe5!? 7 f4 d5 8 Qe2 Bg4 9 Nf3 and Black loses the pinned knight on e5. His attacking possibilities after 9...Bc5!, however, more than compensate.

2) If Black doesn't trust the previous line, there's also the very logical 6...d5!. It's true that 7 exd6 is a discovered check, but following 7...Be6 8 dxc7 Qxc7 Black's development advantage (4-1, with White's queen still exposed) is becoming increasingly menacing. Furthermore, Black even has the very cheeky pseudo-sacrifice 8...Qd1+!? 9 Kxd1 Nxf2+ 10 Ke1 Nxe4 when Black is still miles ahead in development and the c7-pawn will be picked off easily.

5...Be7!

5...Bb4 6 Bd2 0-0 7 0-0-0 Re8 is another logical continuation for Black, but with 5...Be7 Black blocks the e-file and prepares to further annoy the white queen.

6 Bd2 d5!

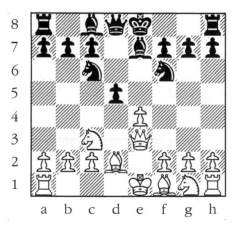

Again exploiting the placing of White's queen, Black forces a liquidation of White's central pawn due to the threat of ...d5-d4, forking queen and knight.

7 exd5 Nxd5

Now White should probably play 8 Nxd5 Qxd5, when both queens are in play. What's interesting, though, is that the liquidation in the centre has actually left Black with a slight development lead (3-2), and this is probably enough to give him an edge overall. Let's see what happens if White tries to improve the position of his queen.

8 Qg3

Now at least the queen is doing something active (attacking the g7-pawn) and it's also no longer in the way of the d2-bishop, but...

8...Ncb4!

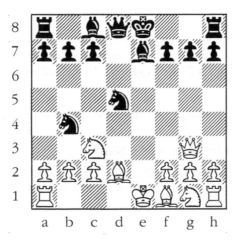

This very strong move introduces a new worry for White, but one that's again based on White's queen: normally it would be the queen's duty to protect the slightly vulnerable c2-pawn, but here that's no longer possible! Now 9 Qxg7? loses to 9...Bf6! followed by ...Nxc2+ and ...Nxa1. White is already struggling here and it's easy to go further astray. Let's see what happened in the game A.Smith-M.Ferguson, British League 2000.

9 0-0-0? Nxc3! 10 bxc3 Nxa2+ 11 Kb2 Be6 12 Ne2 c5

White's king is in a real mess!

13 Nf4 Qb6+ 14 Ka1 Nc1!! 15 Be1

The knight was immune: 15 Bxc1 would have allowed mate in two after 15...Qa5+ 16 Kb2 Qa2. After 15 Be1 Black played 15...Bd6? in the game, but he could have rounded off his previous play in fine style with the move 15...Ba2!!,

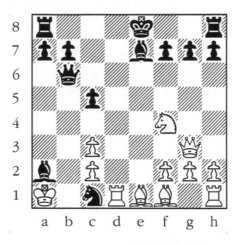

after which White can resign on the spot. The threat is ...Qb1 mate, so 16 Rxc1 is forced, but after 16...Qa5 there is no way to avoid checkmate; for example, 17 Kb2 c4! 18 Rd1 Qa3+ 19 Ka1 Bb3+ 20 Kb1 Qa2+ 21 Kc1 Qxc2 mate!

Now let's take a look at a second example of a queen arriving early on the d4-square.

1 e4 e5 2 Nf3 Nc6 3 Nc3 Nf6 4 d4 exd4 5 Nxd4

We've already seen this position in this chapter, and there we looked at both 5...Bb4 and 5...Bc5. However, isn't it tempting to force White's queen out into the open?

5...Nxd4?! 6 Qxd4

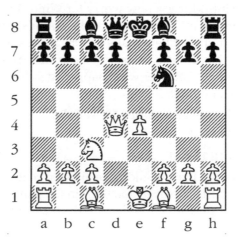

There's certainly some similarities between this position and the one reached after 1 e4 e5 2 d4 exd4 3 Qxd4, but one or two significant differences too. The main change is that Black no longer has the option of attacking the queen with ...Nb8-c6 as this knight is no longer on the board. An associated point is that, with the exchange of a pair of knights, the board is less cluttered than it was at the beginning of the game. Both of these factors add up to leave White's queen being much less vulnerable than in the previous example. And if a queen is actually stable in the middle of the board, this can often be the best place for it; certainly it can demonstrate its full range of powers here.

Another difference between here and the previous example is that there are the added moves ...Ng8-f6 and ...Nb1-c3. This is another plus for White: with the knight still on g8 Black could consider the idea of playing ...Ng8-e7-c6, in effect replacing the knight that's been traded. With the knight on f6, however, Black has to be wary of harassment via e4-e5.

With this is mind, probably Black's best move here is simply 6...d6, taking the sting out of e4-e5, but let's see what could happen if Black insisted on trying to gain time on the queen:

6...b6?

Black prepares to attack the queen with ...Bc5, while the c8-bishop also now has an option of fianchettoing on b7. All well and good in theory, but White can throw a big spanner in the works.

7 e5! Bc5 8 Qf4

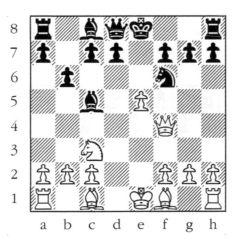

This is a real pain for Black because the knight is struggling for squares, especially since 8...Nh5 allows a double attack with 9 Qf3!.

8...Ng8 9 Bc4!

White goes for mate on f7 scholar's style, but here it's under much more favourable circumstances. In fact, Black is dead lost!

9...Nh6

Or 9...Qe7 10 Nd5! Qd8 11 Nxb6! when the discovered attack threatens both mate on f7 and the rook in the corner.

10 Qf3!

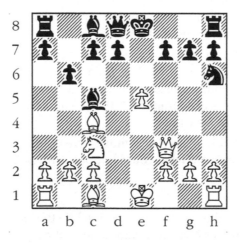

Now White threatens both Qxa8 and, more importantly, Bxh6 followed by Qxf7 mate. Black has no alternative but to give up some material. Not a good advertisement for 6...b6.

Going back to the position after 6 Qxd4, there's a tendency in this position (or in many similar positions) for the inexperienced player to be enticed by **6...c5?!**.

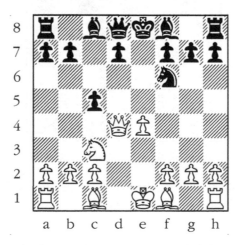

You can understand the attractions to this move: Black gains time by attacking White's queen, and the pawn on c5 certainly contributes towards controlling the centre. So it's often difficult to dissuade a young player from playing in this way.

The trouble for Black is that the negatives outweigh the positives. The problems with this lunge are:

1) Black has permanently weakened the d5- and d6-squares; they can no longer be protected by pawns. The d5-square in particular will no doubt interest White's knight and light-squared bishop, both of which would find it a very welcoming outpost.

2) By playing ...c7-c5 Black has also accepted a backward d-pawn, one that cannot be protected by its neighbours. This problem is magnified by the fact that White can attack the pawn down the half-open d-file.

Let's look at how play could continue:

7 Qe3

Blocking the c1-bishop for the moment, but the queen plans to move to g3.

7...d6

Black would love to be able to liquidate the central pawns with ...d7-d5 but, in contrast to the line we looked at from the Centre Game, this proves to be virtually impossible. After 7...Be7 White could even play 8 e5, as following 8...Ng4 9 Qe4 d6 the check with 10 Bb5+! is very annoying: 10...Bd7 loses to 11 exd6!.

8 Bb5+ Bd7 9 Bxd7+ Qxd7 10 0-0 Be7 11 Qg3 0-0 12 Bh6! Nh5 13 Qf3 Nf6 14 Bf4

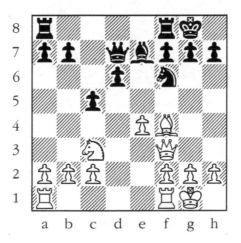

and White will continue with Rad1, adding pressure to the vulnerable d6-pawn; this is a direct consequence of Black's 6th move.

Points to Remember

1) A queen is only vulnerable out in the open if it can be easily attacked.

2) In general, the more exchanges of pieces that have occurred, the more powerful the queen becomes in the centre of the board.

Holding Up and Restricting

So far in this book we've mainly concentrated on positions where both sides develop easily. A typical example of this can be seen if we look at a possible line in our old favourite, the Scotch Game:

1 e4 e5 2 Nf3 Nc6 3 d4 exd4 4 Nxd4 Nf6 5 Nxc6 bxc6 6 Bd3 d5 7 exd5 cxd5 8 0-0 Be7

In a way Black would prefer to develop this bishop more actively on d6 or c5, but he has to be aware of problems resulting from the rook check on e1. For instance, 8...Bd6 9 Re1+! Be6 10 Bb5+! and Black is either forced to move his king or else lose a pawn after 10...Nd7 11 Qxd5; neither of these prospects is particularly enticing.

9 Bf4 0-0 10 Nd2 c6 11 c4 Bg4 12 Qc2 Qb6

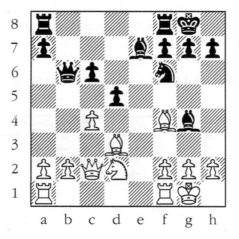

A typical position: both sides have moved freely and after only 12 moves development is more or less complete.

If only development were always as easy! In reality the opening moves of a game often include a mixture of developing your own pieces and both holding up and restricting your opponent's development. For example, after the opening moves...

1 e4 Nc6 2 d4 e5

...White can play...

3 d5

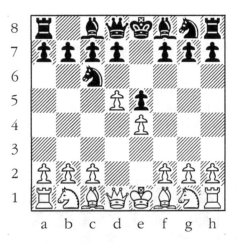

...and Black's development is delayed because he has to spend a tempo doing something about the attack on the c6-knight. Furthermore, after...

3...Nce7

...Black's development is restricted because the knight blocks the dark-squared bishop; it will have to move again (to g6) before the bishop is allowed out.

Question: What's wrong with the move 3...Nd4?

Answer: White can play 4 c3! when the knight is lost because there is no safe retreat square.

Let's now go back to a position we looked at earlier:

1 e4 e5 2 Nf3 Nc6 3 Bb5 a6 4 Ba4 Nf6 5 d3 b5 6 Bb3 Bc5 7 0-0 d6 8 c3 0-0

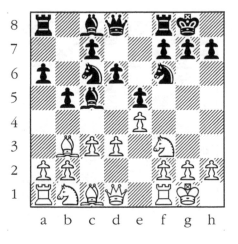

Here I noted that a common idea for White is 9 h3, and in return Black can play 9...h6. These are typical restriction moves that prevent ...Bg4 and Bg5 respectively, the most active locations for these bishops.

Here's an example of restriction occurring earlier on in a game.

1 d4 Nf6

If Black doesn't want to mirror White's first move with 1...d5, this is the main way of preventing White from playing 2 e4. Notice how the first few moves seem to centre on the battle for control of e4.

2 c4 e6 3 Nf3 b6

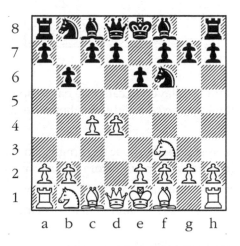

Black prepares to fianchetto on b7. This is known as the Queen's Indian Defence.

4 Nc3 Bb7 5 a3

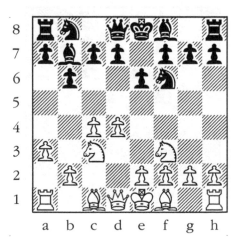

The sole purpose of this move is to prevent ...Bb4, which would pin White's knight and keep control of e4.

Of course there's sometimes a fine line between a restrictive pawn move and an unnecessary pawn move. On this occasion it's believed that it's worth White expending an extra tempo to avoid the active bishop development, or at least this is a worthwhile, if not the only, option.

Now let's go back to the position in the Scotch Game after 5...bxc6:

1 e4 e5 2 Nf3 Nc6 3 d4 exd4 4 Nxd4 Nf6 5 Nxc6 bxc6

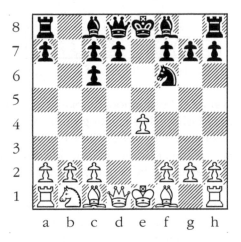

Instead of 6 Bd3, White can make life more difficult by playing the more forceful...

6 e5

...with the idea of holding up Black's development due to the threat on the f6-knight. Of course Black could move the knight here (6...Nd5 and 6...Ne4 are the obvious choices), but he could also carry on the theme of holding up and restricting with the move...

6...Qe7!

...attacking and pinning the e5-pawn, after which White is obliged to spend time dealing with the simple threat of ...Qxe5+. Actually, this is easier said than done. Following 7 Bf4?!, which looks desirable in that White defends e5 by developing a piece, Black can gain time by attacking the bishop with 7...Nd5!; after 8 Bg3 Black could even grab a pawn with 8...Qb4+ 9 Nd2 Qxb2. Instead 7 f4 looks fairly natural, but then Black can pursue his attack on the e5-pawn with 7...d6.

In fact theory considers...

7 Qe2

...to be White's best move, after which Black plays

7...Nd5

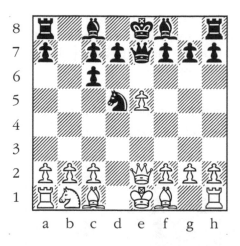

This position is a good example of restriction. By playing 6...Qe7, Black has wilfully blocked in his dark-squared bishop, thus creating problems with his own kingside development. On the other hand, with 7 Qe2 White has been forced to block in his own bishop so he also has trouble finishing off kingside development. The idea behind Black's sophisticated play is that he believes that White will be more inconvenienced by his development problems than Black will be by his. The justification lies in the fact that Black has the upper hand in the standoff between the two queens; Black's queen is free to move whereas White's queen must stay guarding the e5-pawn, at least until it is further defended or Black's queen no longer attacks it.

Sometimes one little pawn move is enough to disrupt an entire development plan.

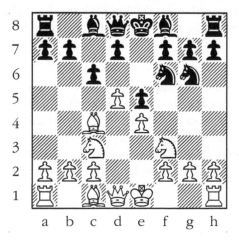

In the above position Black has just played the careless move 6...c6, instead of which either 6...Bc5 or 6...Bb4 followed by ...d7-d6 would have been perfectly fine: Black could castle kingside and would also be ready to develop his light-squared bishop.

After 6...c6, however, White can throw a proverbial spanner in the works with...

7 d6!

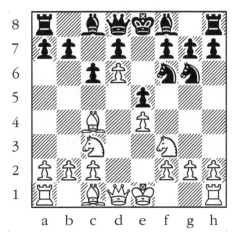

The pawn on d6 cuts Black's position in two and suddenly he has real problems completing development. The bishop on f8 has no moves along the f8-a3 diagonal, and even fianchettoing is problematic – the knight on g6 has to move first, and this is tied up defending the e5-pawn! As a consequence of this, Black will find it extremely difficult to arrange kingside castling. Furthermore, Black also has problems with his queenside, with the only possible development scheme seeming to be ...b7-b5, ...Bb7 and ...Qb6. Even if Black manages to castle queenside, this still doesn't solve the problem of what to do on the other side of the board. The only thing that would really help Black would be to somehow surround and capture the d6-pawn, after which many of his troubles would disappear. Sadly, this is impractical, especially with threats imminent (Ng5!).

Pinning and Unpinning

One of the most typical methods of restriction in the opening is the use of the pin. In most cases this seems to be a bishop pinning a knight to a king or a queen, thus (temporarily at least) preventing the knight in question from taking an active part in the game. Here's a common example:

1 d4 d5 2 c4

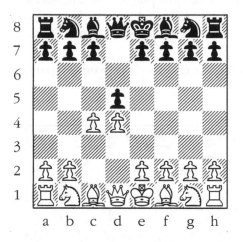

This opening is called the Queen's Gambit, and I'll discuss it in more detail in the next chapter.

2...e6 3 Nc3 Nf6

So far White has been attacking Black's d5-pawn and Black has been solidly defending it.

4 Bg5!

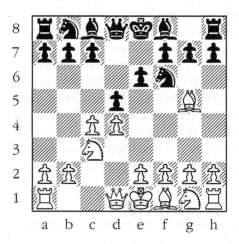

The best move according to theory. Not only does White develop a piece, he also to all extents and purposes disables an enemy piece: if the knight moves, it leaves the queen en prise, so Black can only really move the knight under exceptional circumstances.

Note that the play so far has focussed very much around control of the d5- and e4-

squares – a typical battle for ascendancy in the centre.

Question: What should White play after the move 4...h6?

Answer: White should capture with 5 Bxf6!. The point is that 5...Qxf6 loses a pawn after 6 cxd5 exd5 7 Nxd5. Black could capture with 5...gxf6 but following 6 cxd5 exd5 Black is left with doubled, isolated f-pawns – a real weakness.

After 4 Bg5 Black can solve the problem of the pinned knight with...

4...Be7!

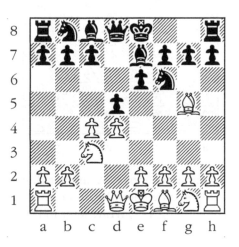

This is an unpinning move. The knight is now free to move (say to e4) because the queen would no longer be under threat; instead there would only be an offer of a trade of bishops. If now 5 Bxf6 Bxf6 Black has nothing to worry about. In contrast to the line 4...h6? 5 Bxf6 Qxf6, the queen on d8 protects d5 so Black doesn't lose a pawn. Instead of 4...Be7, Black could also consider the move 4...Bb4, adding another pin to the game.

Pinning and the Question of Castling

One of the three golden rules of the opening is to ensure king safety. In the majority of cases this means simply tucking up the king safely by castling. However, it's not always quite as simple as that. Sometimes when you castle early you have to be careful not to run into an attack by, say, inviting a pawn storm. Similarly, when the pawn centre is closed and your king is in no immediate danger in the middle of the board, on occasion it pays to keep your options open regarding whether to castle 'short' or 'long'.

The following line shows Black benefiting greatly by the flexibility he has over where his king will eventually decide to go. It's also interesting because it demon-

strates some of the positive and negative aspects of the very common Bg5 and
...Bg4 pins.

1 e4 e5 2 Nf3 Nc6 3 Bc4 Bc5 4 d3

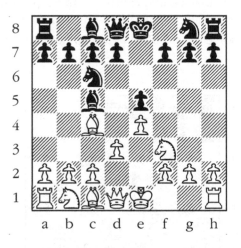

A very solid but rather unambitious move: White has developed the bishop on c4,
so he opens the c1-h6 diagonal to develop the other bishop. In Chapter 6 We'll
take a look at the more challenging 4 c3, while later in this chapter we'll cover the
very aggressive 4 b4!?.

4...Nf6 5 0-0

Given the slow nature of the play, White's king could have hidden behind the central pawns for a couple more moves. However, I do wish to emphasize that 5 0-0
is certainly not a mistake; it's only the follow-up that is faulty.

5...d6 6 Bg5?!

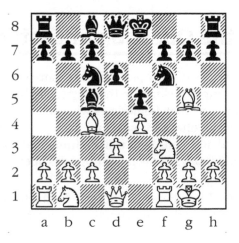

It's incredibly tempting to pin the knight, especially as there is no unpinning device available to Black with ...Be7. However, in this instance it's actually quite a poor idea.

On the other hand, after 6 Nc3 the move 6...Bg4! is quite effective. Let's see what could happen if White followed suit: 7 Bg5 Nd4!

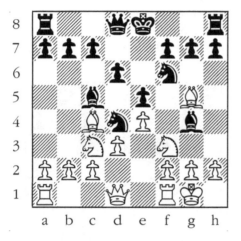

(this is a very desirable follow-up to ...Bg4: pressure increases on White's f3-knight and now White is unable to avoid a wrecked pawn formation in front of his king) 8 Nd5 c6! 9 Nxf6+ gxf6 10 Bh4 (it's true that Black's kingside pawn structure is compromised just as White's will be; the crucial difference is that Black hasn't committed his king to the kingside) 10...Rg8 (even better: Black utilizes the newly-opened file!) 11 Bg3 Qd7 12 c3 Nxf3+ 13 gxf3 Bh3 14 Re1 h5! (threatening to win the pinned bishop with ...h5-h4) 15 Kh1 h4 (anyway!) 16 Bxh4 Bg2+ 17 Kg1 Bxf3+...

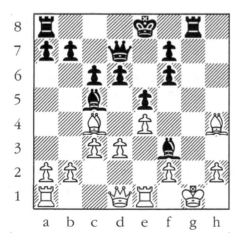

...with a decisive discovered check, winning the white queen.

Instead of 7 Bg5, White should harass the bishop with 7 h3. Following 7...Bh5 White can break the pin with 8 g4 Bg6, but although it must be said the immediate danger has been averted, it's not all good news for White. The extended pawns on the kingside leave White's king rather lacking in cover and open to a later attack.

Of course White could certainly consider playing 6 h3 to avoid 6...Bg4, but there is also a more sophisticated way, one which allows the pin but deals with it very effectively: 6 c3! (preventing ...Nd4 and preparing to challenge the centre in the long run with d3-d4) 6...Bg4 7 Re1 0-0 8 h3 Bh5 9 Nbd2!...

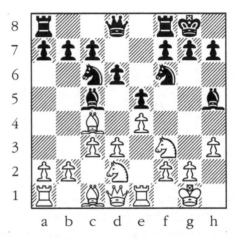

...and White will follow up with the manoeuvre Nd2-f1-g3, attacking the bishop on h5 and forcing Black to make a decision over its future. Black must exchange on f3, allow an exchange on h5 or retreat with ...Bg6: in all cases White solves the problem of the pin.

Getting back to 6 Bg5?!, the question has to be asked, 'why is this dubious, but the pin after 6 Nc3 Bg4! a good idea?' All will become clearer in a couple of moves!

6...h6! 7 Bh4?

White should have played 7 Bxf6 Qxf6 8 Nc3 with the idea of Nd5, or perhaps simply 7 Be3, admitting that 6 Bg5 was a mistake.

7...g5!

Black breaks the pin by lunging forward on the kingside. The crucial difference between this and the line 6 Nc3 Bg4 7 h3 Bh5 8 g4 Bg6 is that Black's king isn't committed to the kingside. It can castle into safety on the queenside or, with the centre being so closed, on this occasion Black's king is safe enough for the moment on the e8-square.

8 Bg3 Bg4!

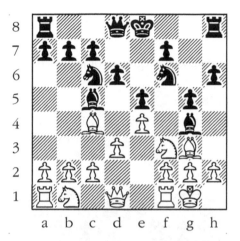

This followed by a queen move and queenside castling gives Black a very promising position. He will gain good attacking chances on the kingside because he has achieved a head start with the tempo-gaining moves ...h7-h6 and ...g7-g5.

This actual position arose in the game H.Jonatansson-B.Halldorsson, Reykjavik 1998. Let's follow it to its conclusion:

9 c3 Bb6 10 Nbd2 Nh5!

The attack begins: Black's plans ...Qf6 and possibly ...Nf4. Meanwhile, in anticipation of Black castling queenside, White gets going on the other wing.

11 b4 Qf6 12 Qb3 Nxg3 13 hxg3 h5!

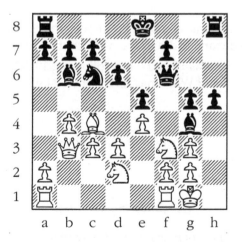

Now ...h5-h4 will blast open the h-file, an especially good idea since Black's rook on h8 will be activated.

14 a4

Threatening to trap the bishop with a4-a5; this is prevented by Black's next move.

14...a5 15 Bd5 h4!

The beginning of a well calculated sequence of moves that brings a decisive attack.

16 gxh4 Bxf3 17 Nxf3 g4! 18 Ng5

After 18 Nh2 Qxh4 White is allowed a check with 19 Bxf7+, but following 19...Kf8 there's no follow-up and White is getting mated down the h-file.

18...Rxh4

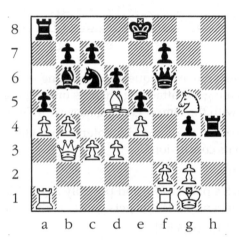

19 Bxf7+

It's seems that White has some counterplay here, but in fact Black has it all under control, and it will be the attack down the h-file that will ultimately be the killer.

Another option for White was 19 Nxf7, but following 19...Qf4! 20 Bxc6+ Black plays the clever 20...Kf8! and White has no defence: 21 g3 Qxg3 is mate due to the pin on the f-pawn.

19...Ke7!

Suddenly White is facing the prospect of Black doubling rooks with ...Rah8, and there is little that can be done about this.

20 Qe6+ Qxe6 21 Bxe6 Rah8! 0-1

(see following diagram)

White threw in the towel as there is no good way to avoid mate down the h-file: after 22 g3 it's mate in two with 22...Rh1+ 23 Kg2 Rhh2.

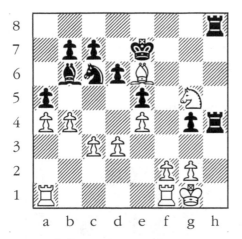

Going back to the position after 8 Bg3, Black can be more than happy with the outcome of the opening after 8...Bg4. However, I can't resist giving another possibility for Black, which I believe was originally played by 19th century World Champion Wilhelm Steinitz. This is certainly more risky but perhaps offers even greater rewards!

8...h5!?

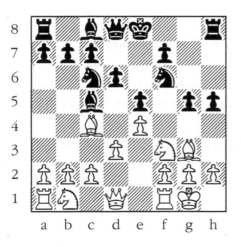

With the strong threat of ...h5-h4, trapping the bishop, but isn't the g5-pawn hanging?

9 Nxg5

Very enticing, especially since the traditionally weak f7-pawn is now hanging.

Steinitz's opponent (Dubois) resisted the temptation of the g-pawn and played the sensible-looking 9 h4 and Steinitz replied with 9...Bg4!. Now if 10 hxg5 Black can press forward with his attack with 10...h4! 11 Bh2 h3! when things are already looking distinctly gloomy for White. One possible continuation is 12 gxf6 Qxf6 13 Nbd2 hxg2 14 Kxg2 0-0-0 15 Bg3 Bh3+ 16 Kg1 Rdg8! when there is no good defence to the devastating threat of ...Rxg3+.

9...h4

Black marches on, ignoring the threat!

10 Nxf7 hxg3!!

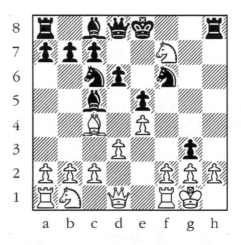

And again! This is a fantastic queen sacrifice.

11 Nxd8 Bg4!

Despite being a queen for a bishop to the good, it's very possible that White is completely lost here: Black's attack is even stronger than it looks.

12 Qd2

Alternatives amply demonstrate Black's winning ideas:

a) 12 Nf7 Rxh2! 13 Qd2 Nd4! 14 Nc3 Nf3+!! 15 gxf3 Bxf3 16 Qh6 (the only move to avoid ...Rh1 mate) 16...Rg2+! 17 Kh1 Rxf2+ 18 Kg1 Rg2+ 19 Kh1 Rg1 mate

b) 12 Nxc6 gxf2+! 13 Kh1 Bxd1 14 Rxd1 Ng4 15 h3 Ne3!.

c) 12 hxg3 Kxd8!! (ignoring the queen) 13 Qd2 Nd4 14 Nc3 Nf3+! 15 gxf3 Bxf3 and there is no defence to ...Rh1 mate.

12...Nd4!

Now Black threatens ...Nd4-e2+ followed by ...Rxh2 mate. White can prevents this, but Black also has another, less obvious, threat.

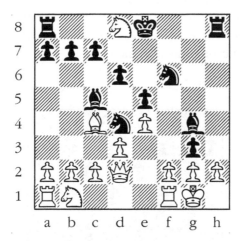

13 Nc3

13 h3 Ne2+ 14 Kh1 allows the beautiful 14...Rxh3+!! 15 gxh3 Bf3 mate. It's true that White can spoil the fun by giving up his queen with 14 Qxe2! although after 14...Bxe2 things still look good for Black.

13...Nf3+!!

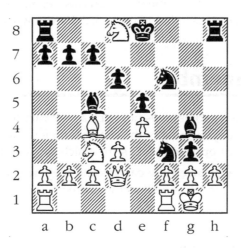

This stunning move, an idea that also cropped up twice in the notes to White's 12th move, is the real justification behind Black's queen sacrifice.

14 gxf3

White is forced to capture because moving the king in the corner allows an immediate checkmate with 14...Rxh2.

14...Bxf3

Now Black threatens mate with ...gxh2, and then ...g1Q if necessary. There is only one way to prevent this, but then another mate becomes available.

Note the major part the bishop on c5 plays here. None of this would have worked had the pawn on f2 not been pinned to the king.

15 hxg3 Rh1 mate!

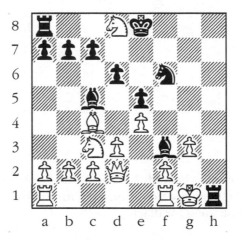

A very nice finish. Given some of the variations above, it's quite understandable why someone would be attracted to playing 8...h5! even when there's a cast-iron alternative in 8...Bg4.

Points to Remember

1) With a closed centre it's sometimes not such a necessity to castle so early. In certain positions leaving your king in the centre for a few more moves can give welcome flexibility: your opponent isn't sure which side to attack.

2) Pins in the opening are powerful weapons and they need to be handled carefully; that's true for the pinner as well as the one being pinned!

Gambits

A gambit is an opening where a player offers to give up material (usually a pawn but sometimes more) in return for some benefits. Usually this advantage consists of one or more of the following:

1) A clear lead in development.

2) Control of the centre.

3) A weakness in the enemy camp.

When deciding on the soundness of a gambit, a player has to weigh up whether these advantages compensate for the material invested. Even if objectively this might not be the case, the gambit may still be worth playing because:

1) In a practical game it's very possible an opponent won't be able to solve the specific problems caused by the gambit.

2) They are great fun to play and lead to very exciting chess!

Perhaps the easiest thing to do here is to pick an example of well-known gambit and illustrate the possibilities it gives:

1 e4 e5 2 Nf3 Nc6 3 Bc4 Bc5 4 b4!?

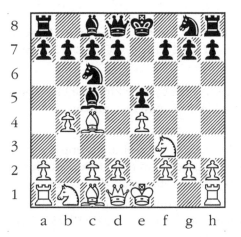

This introduces the Evans Gambit, named after Captain William Davies Evans, the first player known to employ it. In the nineteenth century it was known as a fearsome weapon, with many experts actually suggesting it was the refutation of 3...Bc5. Eventually defensive resources were found for Black and some of its sting has been drawn. Nevertheless, even today it's well respected and has been played by some top grandmasters including Kasparov, Alexander Morozevich and Nigel Short.

4...Bxb4

Of course the thing about many gambits is that they do not necessarily have to be accepted. Here Black can decline the pawn on offer with the simple retreat 4...Bb6.

Question: Following 4...Bb6 can White safely win a pawn after 5 b5 Nd4? 6 Nxe5?

Answer: No! Initially this looks good for White, but Black has a very powerful move in 6...Qg5!,

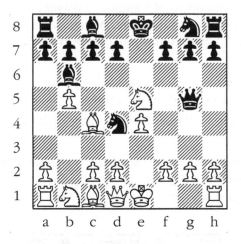

attacking both the knight on e5 and the pawn on g2. Now the tempting 7 Nxf7 loses immediately after 7...Qxg2! 8 Rf1 Qxe4+ 9 Be2 Nf3 mate!

5 c3!

This logical follow-up gains time by attacking the black bishop and also reveals two crucial points behind White's pawn sacrifice:

> 1) c2-c3 prepares to support the desirable central advance d2-d4. White's idea if Black captures with ...exd4 is to recapture with the c-pawn, thus maintaining control with two pawns abreast in the centre.
>
> 2) It also makes way for the queen to develop on the d1-a4 diagonal. In particular, the possibility of Qb3, piling up on Black's f7-pawn, is something both players have to bear in mind.

Add the half-open b-file and the activation of the c1-bishop via a3 or b2 into the mix, and it becomes clear that there's a lot of substance to the Evans Gambit.

5...Ba5

5...Bc5 and ...Be7 are the main alternatives for Black. Of course it's impossible here to give a detailed theoretical overview; I only wish to introduce some of the attacking possibilities that the Evans provides.

6 d4!

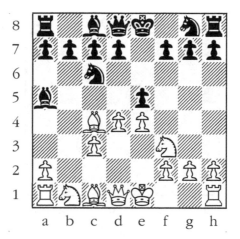

It looked as though Black's previous move made this advance less desirable due to the pin on the a5-e1 diagonal, but White goes ahead anyway!

6 0-0 is of course possible but this does give Black a chance to consolidate with 6...d6! 7 d4 Bb6! (guarding against Qa4 and d4-d5 ideas). Now the continuation 8 dxe5 dxe5 9 Qxd8+ Nxd8 10 Nxe5 regains the pawn, but following 10...Be6 White's initiative has all but expired.

This type of line illustrates well how accurately both sides must play in gambit variations. One slack move by the gambiteer can often see his attack totally fizzle out.

6...exd4

6...d6 is a solid way for Black to play. Now White continues with 7 Qb3 when Black should play the awkward 7...Qd7. The problem with something like 7...Qf6? is that White has the tactic 8 d5! Nce7 9 Qa4+! winning the bishop. The occurrence of these little tricks means that Black must constantly stay on his toes.

7 0-0!

Rapid development is more important than reclaiming one of the pawns. In any case, 7 cxd4 was illegal, and White's idea was never to recapture on d4 with the knight.

7...dxc3

I've given this greedy pawn grab as the 'main line' only to demonstrate the possibilities for White if Black goes astray.

7...Nge7! as a much stronger move, with Black happy to give back one of the pawns in order to complete development and fight for the centre. Following 8 cxd4 Black's idea is to strike back with 8...d5! 9 exd5 Nxd5.

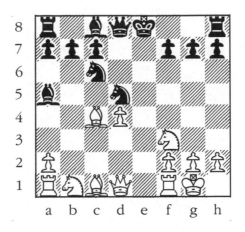

White definitely has some compensation for the pawn here and can increase the pressure with 10 Qb3 Nce7 11 Ba3, but theory considers Black's position to be okay with careful play. It's very useful for Black that the bishop on a5 covers e1, thus ruling out any potentially annoying Re1. Earlier on, a critical alternative for White is 8 Ng5, intending to meet 8...Ne5 with 9 Bxf7+! Nxf7 10 Nxf7 Kxf7 11 Qh5+ and Qxa5.

8 Qb3!

At the moment White is three pawns down, but the first threat arrives and White's pieces are really going to enjoy the open lines.

8...Qf6

8...Qe7 9 Nxc3 also gives White good play for the pawn. Black's difficulties are illustrated by the following high-profile example involving Bobby Fischer: 9...Nf6 10 Nd5! Nxd5 11 exd5 Ne5 12 Nxe5 Qxe5 13 Bb2 Qg5 14 h4! Qxh4 15 Bxg7 Rg8 16 Rae1+ Bxe1 17 Rxe1+ Kd8 18 Qg3!

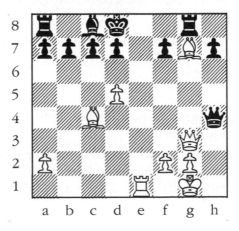

(R.Fischer-R.Fine, USA 1964) and Black resigned in view of the fine finish 18...Qxg3 19 Bf6 mate.

9 e5!

Not giving Black any time to settle.

9...Qg6

9...Nxe5? runs into the pin 10 Re1, and following 10...d6 White wins the bishop with 11 Nxe5 dxe5 12 Qb5+!.

10 Nxc3 Nge7 11 Ba3! 0-0 12 Rad1!

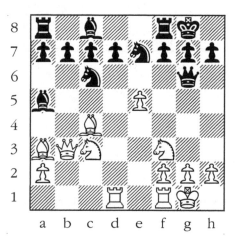

Black has survived the opening few moves and has even managed to castle. However, despite the two-pawn deficit, White's tremendous piece activity would encourage most players to take his side here.

As well as grabbing the material on offer and then 'hanging on', there is another way to approach facing gambits; that is to return some or all of the material in order to diffuse the opponent's initiative. Take the following example:

1 e4 e5 2 d4 exd4 3 c3

This is the Danish Gambit. The 'main line' now continues...

3...dxc3 4 Bc4 cxb2 5 Bxb2

With those bishops pointing towards Black's kingside like trident missiles, this position looks quite frightening from Black's point of view. Those who enjoy facing attacks will happily keep hold of the two pawns and defend grimly. However, many players will prefer to return the material in order to gain time for development. In fact, the main line theory runs...

5...d5!

Development is the key!

6 Bxd5 Nf6! 7 Bxf7+

Has Black missed something?

7...Kxf7 8 Qxd8 Bb4+!

No, this discovered attack means that the queen is regained.

9 Qd2 Bxd2+ 10 Nxd2

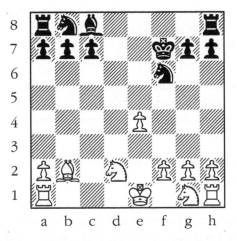

...and the tactical exchanges have led to material equality and a roughly level position.

To keep up the true gambit spirit, White could avoid this simplification with 7

Nc3!?, but at least by returning one of the pawns Black has managed not to fall too far behind in development.

Similarly, earlier Black could have transformed the nature of the position by striking back in the centre with the central thrust 3...d5!?. Following 4 exd5 Qxd5 5 cxd4

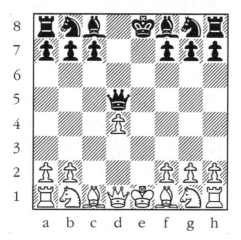

White has regained his pawn, but it's a totally different type of game: Black's development after 5...Nc6 6 Nf3 Bg4 7 Be2 Bb4+ 8 Nc3 is just as rapid and as active as White's.

Never miss a check; it might be mate!

Okay, it probably won't be mate, but it could be just as devastating. Something that inexperienced players are prone to missing in the opening is an important check, especially one that is part of a tactical device. Once an avenue of attack is open to either king, always be wary of any possible checks. Don't forget, checks 'beat' all other threats!

The following 'trick' would catch out quite a few newcomers to the game, and I can say this with some confidence because it's even been known to catch out very experienced players. In fact, on my database of games, I found 79 occurrences of Black losing a piece, and some of the victims' ratings indicated that they were very strong club players!

1 e4 c5

The Sicilian Defence, which cropped up in Chapter 1. We'll discuss it in more detail in Chapters 5 and 6.

2 Nf3 d6 3 c3 Nf6 4 Be2

Question: Isn't there a pawn that Black can grab here?

Answer: Let's see...

4...Nxe4?? 5 Qa4+!

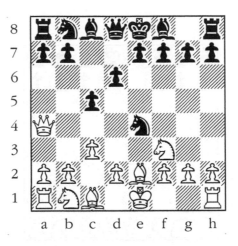

Check! Black has to block the a4-e8 diagonal and White will simply follow up with Qxe4, leaving him a piece for a pawn to the good.

Patzer sees a check!

On the other end of the scale, there's the well-known term in chess circles, 'Patzer sees a check; patzer plays a check.' In the opening it's tempting to develop a piece with check because this seemingly gains time. However, if the opponent has a beneficial way to get out of check, often the check isn't worth giving in the first place. For example:

1 e4 e5 2 Nf3 Nc6 3 d4

It's the Scotch again! So far we've only looked at examples where Black deals with the attack on e5 by exchanging pawns in the centre, but why not throw in a check first?

3...Bb4+? 4 c3!

That's why! Instead of gaining time, Black actually loses time because the bishop is forced to retreat, and White has gained the useful move c2-c3. What's worse for Black is that to protect the pawn on e5, the bishop is forced to move to a very unfortunate square.

4...Bd6

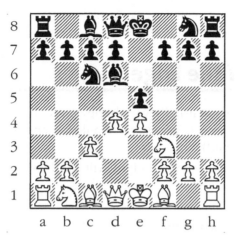

We've talked about the problem of the bishop being developed in front of the d-pawn before. It's a pretty grim situation, for this bishop and even more so for the one on c8!

In this next example, Black plays the same check (...Bb4), but under much more favourable circumstances.

1 d4 Nf6 2 c4 e6 3 Nf3 Bb4+

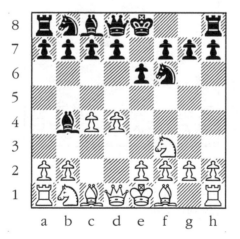

Here the big difference is that White's c-pawn has already advanced to c4, so there is no option for White to gain time by attacking the bishop with c2-c3. White must block with either the knight or bishop (4 Nc3, 4 Nbd2 or 4 Bd2). After knight moves Black is free to carry on developing, while after 4 Bd2 Black could trade bishops and again continue developing or else protect the bishop (4...a5, 4...c5 or 4...Qe7 are the usual ways to do this). So 3...Bb4+ is a perfectly acceptable move and is known as the Bogo-Indian Defence.

Springing off the Edge

It's true that knights are not usually very happy pieces on the edge of the board, but that doesn't mean to say this scenario should be completely avoided (guidelines, not rules, remember!).

There are quite a few cases where a knight will use the side of the board as a stepping stone to greener pastures:

1 d4 Nf6 2 c4 e5!?

This is called the Budapest Gambit.

3 dxe5 Ng4 4 e3

White could try to hang onto the extra pawn, but here he prefers to simply give it back.

4...Nxe5

Here White could play the natural 5 Nf3, offering an exchange of knights. However, there's also nothing wrong with...

5 Nh3!?

If White were to leave the knight on this square, then this would be a poor idea, but the intention is to follow up with Nf4. On the f4-square the knight is doing a good job controlling a key central point d5, a square White can dominate after playing Nf4 and Nc3.

Here's another example:

1 Nf3 d5 2 c4 dxc4

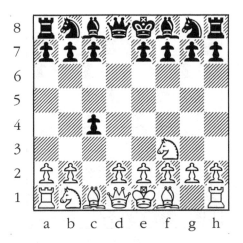

White should have no qualms about playing the move **3 Na3** here. After all, the knight is only on a very short stop on a3; next move it plans to capture the pawn on c4.

Exercises

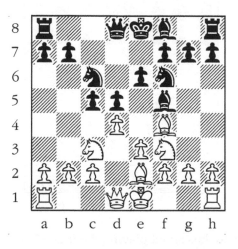

1) In this position White can play **7 Nb5** with the threat of Nc7+, winning an exchange. Is this a good idea?

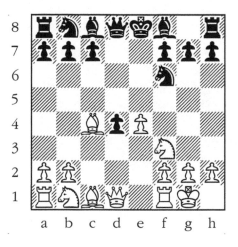

2) In this position Black, already a pawn ahead, has the option of grabbing White's e-pawn with **6...Nxe4**. Is winning this central pawn worth the risk involved?

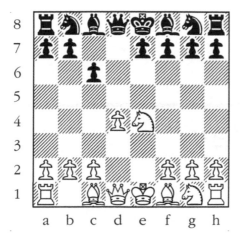

3) The main line of the Caro-Kann Defence begins **1 e4 c6 2 d4 d5 3 Nc3 dxe4 4 Nxe4**. In this position, can you suggest two ways for Black to develop with threats and on each occasion consider White's replies?

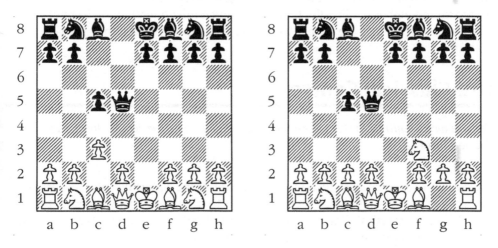

4) Here are two positions that could arise from the Sicilian Defence. Explain briefly why one is commonly seen in tournament play whereas the other is hardly ever witnessed.

Chapter Five

Pawn Play

So far we've concentrated mainly on pieces and how they should develop, whereas the role of the pawns in the opening has been somewhat neglected. In this chapter I'm hoping to redress the balance by studying a few basic pawn structures arising from the opening before moving on to some typical pawn breaks that are worth remembering. Finally, there's the much misunderstood subject of doubled pawns: when they are a clear weakness compared to when they prove to be a strength.

The Classical Centre

The side which controls the centre automatically enjoys more freedom for his pieces. – Reuben Fine

In Chapter 1 we were introduced to the concept of the classical centre and its advantages. Now I want to talk a bit more about this, and especially the possibilities of building the classical centre in 1 e4 and 1 d4 openings, assuming Black prevents an immediate set-up, e.g. by playing 1 e4 e5 or 1 d4 d5.

Building the Classical Centre after 1 e4 e5

The diagram above shows a fundamental pawn structure that could easily arise via 1 e4 e5. White has created the classical centre by playing the preparatory pawn move c2-c3, which has supported the central advance d2-d4. The point is that if Black were to trade pawns on d4 with...

1...exd4

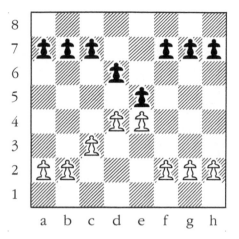

...then White is in a position to maintain the classical centre with...

2 cxd4

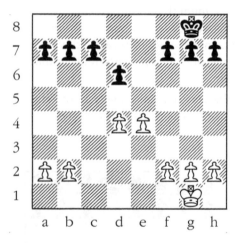

Now we have reached a pawn structure that is known to be very favourable for White due to his extra space and control of the centre. Unless Black is able to put this classical centre under real pressure by attacking it with pieces, he is more likely to refrain from playing ...exd4, preferring to keep the tension in the position; the pawn on e5 is, after all, defended with ...d7-d6.

In turn White has the option of exchanging pawns on e5 with the move dxe5, but it's clear that after the recapture ...dxe5 Black has as much presence in the centre as White. Thus White is also often reluctant to release the tension.

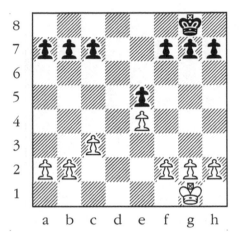

The Timing of c2-c3

Let's just suppose for a moment that White definitely wishes to create a classical pawn centre after 1 e4 e5 (we've already seen openings, such as the Scotch Game, where White's concern is more to do with rapid development), and that the move c2-c3 obviously comes into play at some moment. In that case the timing of this advance is very important.

Let's first of all look at the very extreme case where White puts this idea above everything else and plays c2-c3 as early as move two.

1 e4 e5 2 c3

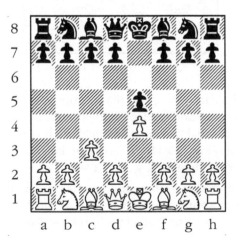

Perfectly logical play of course: White wants to play d2-d4 as soon as possible. Indeed the great Paul Morphy, arguably the strongest player of the 19th century, played this at least once.

Question: Can you find two weaknesses of the move 2 c3?

Answer: Firstly, it doesn't do much for White's development and, secondly, it deprives the b1-knight of its favourite square.

There's also a third point that's equally important: unlike 2 Nf3 it doesn't create a direct threat, so Black isn't forced onto the back foot. Played so early on in the game, a non-developing and non-threatening move such as c2-c3 gives Black the opportunity to grab the initiative:

2...Nf6!

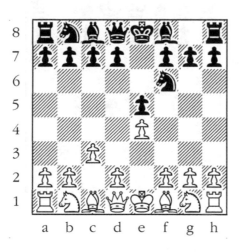

Suddenly White's previous move doesn't look so attractive. Black immediately attacks the e4-pawn just at a time when the natural defensive move Nc3 is out of the question.

The problem for White is that there is no obvious way to both defend e4 and keep the d2-d4 dream alive, for example:

a) The most obvious way to protect the e4-pawn is with 3 d3, but this rather contradicts White's previous move, and certainly the idea of d4 has to be put onto the back-burner for a while, or perhaps for good if Black follows up energetically with 3...d5!.

b) 3 Qc2 is idealistic but before White is able to play d2-d4 Black gets in first. Following 3...d5! 4 exd5 Qxd5! it's an occasion where the queen is well placed in the centre: there's no Nc3 to harass it, while (with different colours) we saw in Chapter 4 the structural problems associated with playing c3-c4 here. In short, Black is doing well after 4...Qxd5.

c) I would hope by now that you would be quick to reject both 3 f3?! and 3 Bd3?! for reasons we've spoken about before. In each case 3...d5! is again a good answer. When all is said and done, the only really challenging move for White is...

3 d4

...even if Black can immediately eliminate one pawn in White's central pairing:

3...Nxe4

Question: What does White play after 3...exd4 here?

Answer: 4 e5! followed by cxd4.

4 dxe5

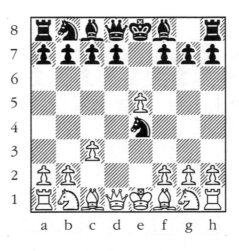

4...d5!

The safest move. In the Morphy game I mentioned (versus. A.Bottin, Paris 1858) the young American showed his legendary attacking skills against the tempting 4...Bc5!? after 5 Qg4!? Nxf2? (5...Bxf2+ 6 Kd1 d5 7 Qxg7 Rf8 should be played) 6 Qxg7! Rf8 7 Bg5! f6 8 exf6 Rxf6 (8...Nxh1 9 Be2! and Bh5+ will be crushing) 9 Bxf6 Be7 10 Qg8+ and Black resigned.

After 4...d5 Black has a very comfortable position and this is the reason why 2 c3 is hardly ever seen in tournament chess. 5 f3? loses material to 5...Qh4+! 6 g3 Nxg3!, and it's difficult to get rid of Black's knight without playing...

5 exd6

...but after...

5...Nxd6

...Black can even claim to be slightly ahead in development in this position without any central pawns.

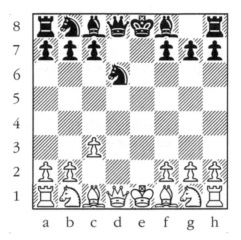

Question: Why is 5...Bxd6 not a stronger option for Black than 5...Nxd6?

Answer: White wins a piece with 6 Qa4+!. Never miss a check!

Let's look at an example where White delays the plan of c2-c3 and d2-d4, only opting for it at a more suitable moment.

1 e4 e5 2 Nf3 Nc6 3 Bb5

The Ruy Lopez, which we've already come across in Chapters 2 and 4.

3...a6 4 Ba4 Nf6 5 0-0 b5 6 Bb3 Bb7

In Chapter 4 we examined the possibility of grabbing the pawn with 6...Nxe4. Here Black chooses a safer alternative. Those who are keen to attach a name to each line should call this the Archangel Variation.

7 Re1!

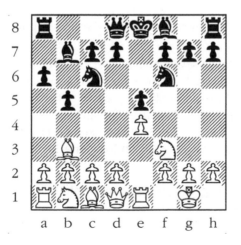

The difference between this and the previous example is that with 7 Re1 White has found an economical way to protect the e4-pawn; crucially one that doesn't interfere with the natural process of establishing the classical pawn centre with c2-c3 and d2-d4. Because White has already developed a few pieces and castled quickly, Black is in a less favourable position if he tries to take over the initiative in the centre.

7...Bc5

More active than 8...Be7, although the flipside is that 8...Bc5 does rather walk straight into White's main plan (see the next note).

8 c3!

There's no reason to hesitate now, and there's the added bonus that d2-d4 will gain time by attacking the bishop.

8...d6!

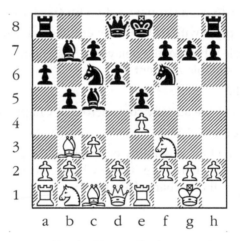

Black prepares to base his defence around the solid support of the e5-pawn – a very sensible option.

In the previous example we saw Black answering c2-c3 with a very quick ...d7-d5, taking the initiative in the centre. However, in this particular position, the idea is unfeasible, After 8...d5? 9 exd5 Nxd5 we see one of the hidden points of Re1: it doesn't only defend the e5-pawn, it also discourages Black from central activity such as this. Following 10 Nxe5 0-0 11 Nxc6 Bxc6 12 d4 White is a good pawn ahead, while 10 d4!, exploiting the pin on the e-file, is probably even stronger.

9 d4 Bb6!

The right follow-up to the previous move, with Black holding firm in the centre. 9...exd4 10 cxd4 reaches a structure which, as I mentioned earlier, is usually very favourable for White unless Black can quickly put the centre under pressure.

10 Be3

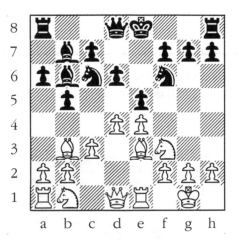

Taking steps to protect his prize asset: the centre (the more aggressive 10 Bg5 also looks sensible). This position has been reached many, many times in tournament play. White's centre gives him an edge, but Black is very solid and has no real reason to complain either.

Question: White's bishop has just blocked the rook's defence of the e4-pawn. Should Black take advantage by grabbing the e-pawn on offer with 10...Nxe4?

Answer: Certainly not! Following 11 d5! White wins a piece due to uncovered attacks on the e4-knight (I'll leave it to you to check the variations). Again we see the power of the e1-rook!

A typical continuation is 10...0-0 11 Nbd2 (defending e4) 11...h6 (preventing Bg5 or Ng5, and thus preparing ...Ng4 followed by ...Nxe3) 12 h3

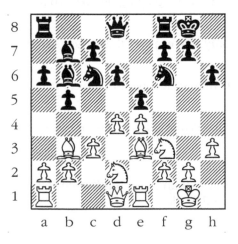

(preventing ...Ng4) and so on. One can see by the moves played the emphasis both sides place on the central battle.

The Sicilian

The other way Black can prevent an immediate classical centre after 1 e4 by preparing to trade pawns is the Sicilian Defence:

1 e4 c5

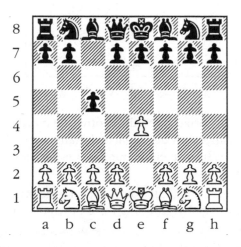

As I mentioned in Chapter 1, the Sicilian is the most popular and widely-played opening in the history of chess. The reason for its huge popularity is the widely held belief that it allows Black to play for a win without unjustified risks. From the very first move Black sharply unbalances the position by creating an asymmetrical pawn structure. Let's continue by playing one or two natural moves:

2 Nf3 d6

This certainly isn't the only move, as we'll discover in Chapter 6.

3 d4

White plays in 'Scotch Game' style, opening the centre very quickly.

3...cxd4!

Exchanging the c-pawn for White's d-pawn is an essential part of the Sicilian's strategy.

4 Nxd4 Nf6 5 Nc3 e6

Again Black has moves other than 5...e6, but I've chosen this for the moment to illustrate best the structural battle.

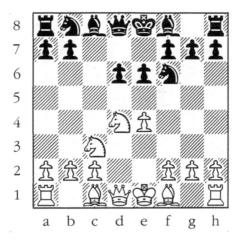

The group of variations where White plays an early d2-d4 and, after the exchange of pawns, recaptures with the knight is called the Open Sicilian. The first thing to notice about the diagram is that White can certainly develop more freely than Black; both his bishops, for example, have a wide range of options, whereas Black's are more limited. Black, however, has a very subtle structural advantage, one that is very difficult to appreciate at first sight. The advantage he has is his superior control of the critical central squares due to his d- and e-pawns. Note here that they control the squares f5, e5, d5 and c5; White's solitary pawn on e4 only controls d5 and f5 – half the number of squares! A simplistic view, perhaps, but it's factors like this which really attract players to the Sicilian.

Building a Classical Centre against the Sicilian

Of course, just as after 1 e4 e5, White isn't forced to play 2 Nf3 followed by an immediate d2-d4. There's certainly an argument for trying to build a centre with c2-c3 and d2-d4. So, just as with 1 e4 e5, let's take a brief look at White attempting to do this, beginning with the immediate...

1 e4 c5 2 c3

(see following diagram)

This is unimaginatively named the c3 Sicilian. If Black continues with something non-threatening such as 2...d6, 2...e6 or 2...Nc6, White will certainly reply with 3 d4.

Question: Can you suggest two natural ways for Black to try to exploit the non-developing nature of White's second move?

Answer: With either 2...d5! or 2...Nf6!.

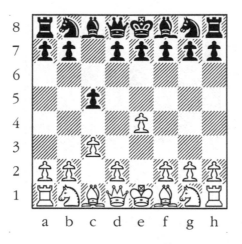

Note that both of these moves play on the fact that White can no longer develop the queen's knight on c3 as the pawn is in the way. Let's examine each in turn:

a) 2...d5

Directly attacking e4. Normally White would be reasonably happy to force Black's queen into the centre, but following...

3 exd5 Qxd5

...the problem is that the most natural way to harass the queen to gain time, Nc3, is impossible and so Black's queen is fairly comfortably placed in the centre (I only say 'fairly' because Black still has to be careful). White can stake some claim for the centre with...

4 d4

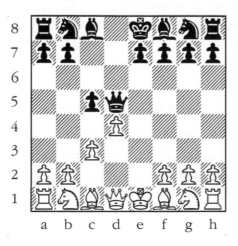

...but with the e-pawn off the board White obviously won't be dominating the centre. There are plenty of ways the game could continue from here, and this book certainly isn't the place to reproduce the oodles of theory. Instead I'll content myself with just giving a logical sequence of development:

4...Nf6 5 Nf3 Bg4 6 Be2 e6 7 0-0 Nc6

...etc. with a level position.

b) 2...Nf6

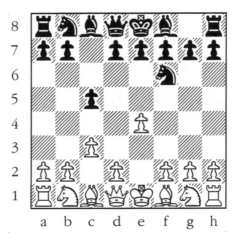

This exploits White's second move in similar way: White can no longer protect e4 in the most natural way with Nc3. If White protects the pawn on e4 in order to keep his hopes alive of a classical centre, he is forced to make a concession, for example:

a) 3 d3, though not bad, is not ideal because the pawn really wants to go to d4 in one go.

b) 3 Bd3!? breaks a cardinal rule in that it blocks the d-pawn. In fact here it's not so bad, as White plans Bd3-c2 followed by d2-d4. It's probably a bit too slow to really give White a plus, even though play is interesting after, say, 3...Nc6 4 Nf3! (4 Bc2 d5 shatters White's plans) 4...d5 5 e5 Ng4 6 Qe2 c4 7 Bc2 Qc7 8 Ba4.

c) 3 Qc2!? defends e4 and therefore has some logic to it, but somehow it looks unnatural and White must be careful his queen doesn't get harassed. A cautionary tale was provided in the game C.Cave-H.Urday Caceres, Elista Olympiad 1998 after 3...Nc6 4 Nf3 e6 5 d4 cxd4 6 cxd4 Nb4! 7 Qe2 (the only way to stay protecting e4, even if the queen is unfortunately placed, blocking the f1-bishop) 7...d5! 8 e5 Ne4! 9 a3?? Qc7! (attacking c1 as well as threatening ...Nc2+) 10 Kd1 Nd3!!...

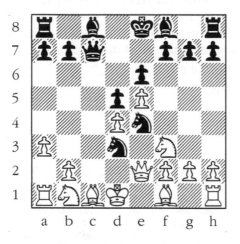

...when White could have quite easily resigned here and now, especially as 11 Be3 Nexf2+! 12 Bxf2 allows mate with 12...Qc1, while 11 Qxd3 Nxf2+ is a winning 'family' fork.

Okay, so White has ways of defending e4, but nothing really convincing. Instead White's most popular choice here by an overwhelming margin is...

3 e5!

It's not difficult to see why either. White turns Black's threat on its head and it's now Black having to deal with a threat: good, logical opening play.

3...Nd5

The best square. 3...Ne4?? loses the knight after 4 d3!.

4 d4 cxd4 5 cxd4

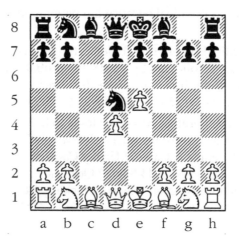

Okay, White has some form of central pawn formation (he has at least kept both e- and d-pawns), and in a way it looks more menacing than the classical centre due to the advanced nature of the e-pawn. But in fact as it stands the centre is not quite so strong because:

1) It covers fewer central squares.
2) It leaves Black with an outpost on d5, conveniently taken up by the knight.
3) It is more prone to attack.

Regarding the final point, Black can choose immediate action against White's centre with...

5...d6

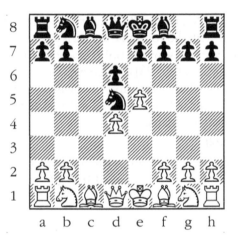

...when one of White's pawn duo is likely to be exchanged in the next few moves.

Perhaps I'm painting too bleak a picture. It's not all doom and gloom for White, and this is certainly a very playable line from White's point of view. I'm just trying to illustrate it's not possible to create the classical centre after 2 c3 if Black develops dynamically.

Let's now look at some possibilities if, as in the Ruy Lopez, White delays playing c2-c3 and instead concentrates on rapid development before building the centre.

1 e4 c5 2 Nf3 d6

One of the points of this move is to prepare ...Nf6 without the possibility of this knight being kicked away with e4-e5.

3 Bb5+

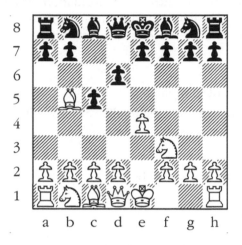

After 3 Bc4 Black does well to attack White's e-pawn immediately before White has a chance to defend it with 0-0 followed by Re1: 3...Nf6! 4 Qe2 (of course 4 d3 and; 4 Nc3 are possible, but for now I'm only concentrating on moves that keep up the idea of a quick c2-c3 and d2-d4) 4...Nc6 5 c3 Bg4! (preventing 6 d4) 6 0-0 e6 7 Rd1 Be7 8 d4 cxd4 9 cxd4 (finally creating the desired centre but...) 9...d5! 10 exd5 Nxd5 and Black has immediately managed to trade off one of the pawns leaving him with a comfortable game.

3...Bd7 4 Bxd7+ Qxd7 5 0-0

Now at least White can answer ...Nf6 with Re1 which, as we saw in the Ruy Lopez, seems the most natural way to defend e4 if White is aiming for c2-c3 and d2-d4.

5...Nc6 6 c3 Nf6 7 Re1

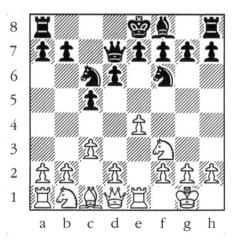

All is set for the construction of the classical centre. What should Black do?

7...e6! 8 d4 cxd4 9 cxd4 d5!

Fighting back in the centre. In the Ruy Lopez example we saw Black basing his strategy around supporting his e5-pawn; here he does something similar but with the d-pawn. The point here is that White cannot keep the classical centre as there is no way to protect the e4-pawn with f2-f3. White must either advance to e5 or trade one of his central duo.

10 e5 Ne4

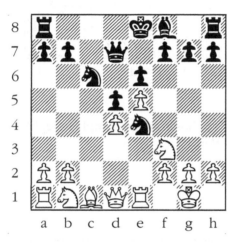

The tension has gone in the centre and it's become closed with a French Defence structure (more on this later in the chapter). It's a sensible idea for White to challenge Black's strong knight with 11 Nbd2 when play typically continues 11...Nxd2 12 Bxd2 Be7 with a roughly equal position.

Pawn Play with 1 d4 d5

Time for a change! I know that 1 e4 openings have dominated the proceedings so far (and I make no apologies for that!) but now it's time to look at some pawn play after 1 d4 d5. It will soon become clear that there are one or two important differences between this and the action after 1 e4 e5. The main difference is seen when White tries to create a classical centre. Just as with 1 e4 e5 and 1 e4 c5, let's go through the same process and look at a few examples:

1 d4 d5 2 f3

Immediately going for the classical centre with e2-e4. But those who have read Chapter 3 (I hope you all have!) know that the f2-f3 should signal the ringing of some alarm bells.

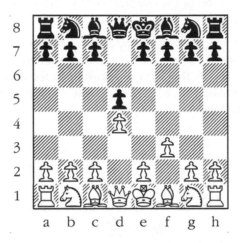

2...e6

Not the best move, but I've chosen it here simply to highlight one of the problems with the f2-f3 and e2-e4 plan.

3 e4?! dxe4! 4 fxe4?

Classical centre achieved...

4...Qh4+!

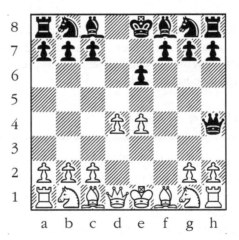

...for all of one move, as ...Qxe4 is up next!

Pretty disastrous for White, even more so if he insists on playing 5 g3? after which 5...Qxe4+ nets the rook on h1.

So, point taken: if White wants to play f2-f3 and e2-e4 he has to be careful about problems with king safety. Let's now try a similar, but more circumspect, approach:

1 d4 d5 2 Nc3 Nf6 3 f3

Now that the moves Nc3 and Nf6 have been inserted, there are fewer problems to worry about based on ...Qh4+ tricks, so White feels more justified in trying for e2-e4. However...

3...c5!

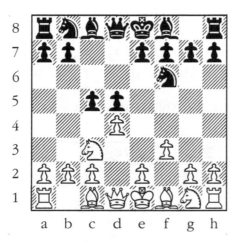

Throughout the next few pages I hope you'll begin to appreciate the vital role the c-pawn lunge plays in 1 d4 openings. Crucially, with this move Black has been the one to strike first, and White's hopes of creating the classical centre have been shattered.

Question: Can't White win a pawn here with the obvious 4 dxc5?

Answer: Yes, temporarily, but he cannot hang onto it.

In fact after 4 dxc5? Black can grab the advantage with 4...d4! when having to move the knight is very awkward for White.

(see following diagram)

Here are the options:

a) 5 Nb5? loses the knight to 5...Qa5+! and ...Qxb5.

b) 5 Na4 protects the c5-pawn for the moment, but after 5...Qa5+! White's only move to keep the knight is 6 c3. However, White's position remains precarious after 6...Bd7! 7 b3 (what else?) 7...Bxa4 8 bxa4 dxc3 when Black has regained his pawn and others (c5) are likely to follow.

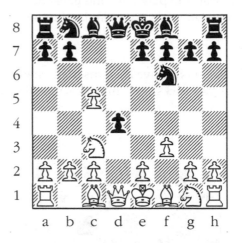

c) 5 Nb1 is very depressing for White, and after 5...e5!

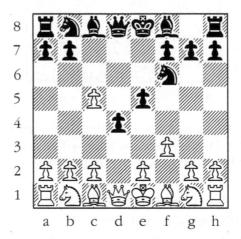

(threatening ...Bxc5) it's Black who has taken over the centre. Added to this White's lag in development and the weakening f3 and it's clear the opening has been a bit of a disaster. If White could hang onto his extra pawn, all would not be lost, but sadly this is impossible. If 6 b4 Black replies with 6...a5! breaking the pawn chain before White has a chance to consolidate. I'll leave you to work out why White loses his pawn; suffice to say that 7 a3 doesn't help as 7...axb4 exploits the pin on the a-file.

d) 5 Ne4 offers a trade of knights, and following 5...Nxe4 6 fxe4 e5 Black will once more regain his pawn with a very nice position (7 b4 is met by 7...a5!) Note that ...Qh4+ is suddenly a possibility again.

Going back to White's fourth move, it's clear that White should refrain from 4 dxc5, but what else? 4 e3 supports the d4-pawn but is clearly a compromise after the initial grandiose plan of e2-e4. Following 4...Nc6 the move f2-f3 looks more than a little silly if White isn't playing e4. Note that 5 dxc5 still doesn't win a pawn: 5...e5 6 Na4 and amongst others, Black can even use the trick 6...Bxc5 7 Nxc5 Qa5+ 8 c3 Qxc5...

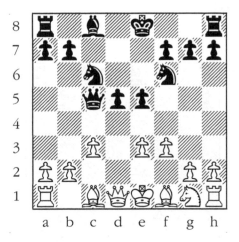

...when a development count reveals a very poor showing for White.

In fact, in the absence of useful alternatives, it seems that after 3...c5! White's best bet is to go 'all in' with...

4 e4!

The idea is to offer a pawn sacrifice after 4...dxe4 with 5 d5! exf3 6 Nxf3. Of course Black could go down this route, but another promising continuation is...

4...cxd4 5 Qxd4 Nc6

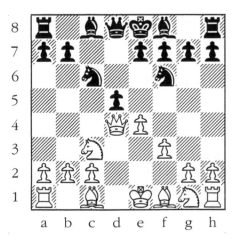

6 Bb5

Otherwise White must lose time with his queen and Black would follow up with ...d5-d4!.

6...Bd7 7 Bxc6 Bxc6 8 e5

At least this way White keeps one central pawn. 8 exd5 Nxd5 9 Nge2 e6 is more than comfortable for Black.

8...Nd7 9 f4 e6

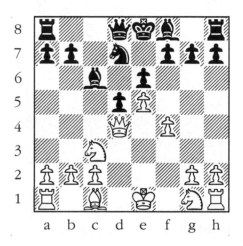

...and Black will continue with ...Bc5, gaining time on the white queen. The game S.Warkentin-O.Korneev, Le Touquet 1993 continued 10 Nf3 Bc5 11 Qd3 Qb6 when one of the problems with White's position was that kingside castling was ruled out. In any case, this probably isn't the kind of position White was envisaging when playing 3 f3.

Before disregarding the plan of f2-f3 and e2-e4 completely, I want to look at a line where White delays it a move further.

1 d4 d5 2 Nc3 Nf6 3 Bg5

A mirror image of the Ruy Lopez – seems pretty logical. In fact this opening has a name: the Veresov.

3...Nbd7

Black has other playable moves (3...Bf5 is sensible, and 3...c5!? is more adventurous) but this is the traditional main line. It might seem a little odd to block the c8-bishop, but on the other hand if White captures on f6 Black now has the option of recapturing with the knight. Also, on d7 the knight supports the ...c7-c5 advance, and we saw how powerful that was in the previous example.

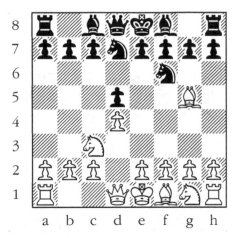

Let's see what happens if White again goes for f2-f3:

4 f3 c5!

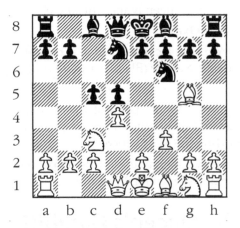

White is slightly more favourably placed here than in the previous example (not difficult really!), but this is still the move to play.

5 e4!

Again rapidly opening lines is the best course. 5 dxc5 is certainly more playable here than in the previous example because there is no ...d5-d4 and Black has to watch his d5-pawn. However, theory considers Black's chances to be good after 5...e6, planning to regain the pawn. For example: 6 b4 h6 7 Bh4 b6! (not giving White the chance to consolidate) 8 c6 Ne5 and now if White tries to keep hold of his extra pawn with 9 b5, then 9...Bb4 is strong: 10 Qd4 Nc4 11 Rb1 e5! 12 Qd3 Bf5! 13 Qxf5 Bxc3+ 14 Kf2 Bd4+ looks horribly unpleasant for White.

5...cxd4

5...dxe4 is also possible, when White offers a pawn sacrifice with 6 d5.

6 Qxd4 e5!

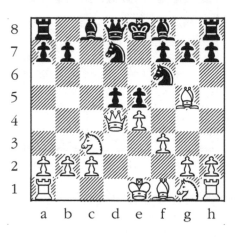

Of course! Gaining time on the queen makes this the obvious choice.

7 Qa4 d4 8 Nd5 Be7 9 Nxe7 Qxe7

Okay, not a disaster for White (in fact the position is roughly level), but not exactly world domination in the centre either (Black has more central pawn presence).

Another annoying thing from White's point of view is that there's no equivalent of the Scotch Opening after 1 d4 d5 because, in contrast to 1 e4 e5 2 Nf3 Nc6 3 d4, there is no queen supporting the e4 advance.

So just how is White supposed to play these 1 d4 d5 positions? Is he resigned to the fact that there is no real pawn action? Not quite...

Introducing the Queen's Gambit!

1 d4 d5 2 c4!

This is the Queen's Gambit – White gives Black the opportunity to capture a pawn. However, strictly speaking this is not a true gambit like the ones discussed in the previous chapter because Black isn't able to hold on to his extra pawn.

After all the hassle White was experiencing trying to arrange an effective e4 in the previous examples, it should become clear what White's basic strategy is here: the aim is simply to get rid of the d5-pawn so that the opposition to the e4 advance suddenly disappears.

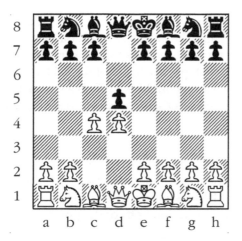

There's obviously considerable choice for both sides, but let's just see what happens if Black accepts the pawn offer, White tries to regain it immediately and Black doesn't play ball:

2...dxc4

This is unsurprisingly called the Queen's Gambit Accepted.

3 e3

Again not the only move (4 e4 and 4 Nf3 are also played), but useful for this demonstration. With 3 e3 White adds support to the d4-pawn and plans to recapture with Bxc4. Let's see what could happen if Black grimly tries to hold on to this pawn.

3...b5?! 4 a4! c6? 5 axb5 cxb5? 6 Qf3!

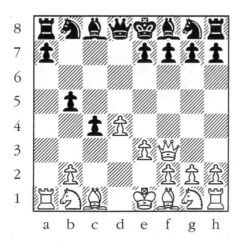

Oops! The only way to avoid losing the rook is with 6...Nc6, but then White simply captures with 7 Qxc6+.

3...Be6 is better than 3...b5, but it's still ugly (the f8-bishop has a right to complain) and in any case 4 Na3 regains the pawn by force. Black can achieve a perfectly reasonable position as long as he realizes that he cannot hang onto his pawn. Instead he should simply develop with 3...Nf6 4 Bxc4. Here he shouldn't be tempted by 4...Bg4?, as 5 Qb3!, attacking both b7 and f7, is a strong reply. Instead Black should be content with 5...e6, after which he can strike back in the centre with the pawn break ...c7-c5

Now that it's established there are no worries about White losing a pawn with the Queen's Gambit, let's have a look at how the pawn play in this opening influences the battle for the centre. The following game, from a simultaneous display given by Garry Kasparov, is an illustration both of the power of the Queen's Gambit and of central domination.

G.Kasparov-J.Rebelo
Lisbon 1999

---

1 d4 d5 2 c4 e6

The most solid reply – Black refuses to give any ground away in the centre. If White captures on d5 then Black is ready to recapture with the pawn, thus keeping control of the important central squares.

3 Nc3

Again sensible play – White develops the knight to its normal square and adds pressure to the centre.

3...Nf6 4 cxd5 Nxd5

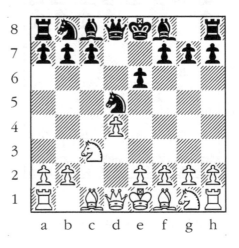

Although it would perhaps be a little harsh to call this a genuine mistake, it does rather give White a free hand in the centre and it kind of justifies White's opening. More consistent is 4...exd5!, preserving a grip on the e4-square and thus preventing White from continuing with e2-e4.

5 e4 Nf6?!

This is definitely an error as it loses valuable time. Black should play 5...Nxc3 6 bxc3 c5!, attacking White's centre.

6 Nf3 h6?!

This unquestionably comes under the 'unnecessary pawn move' category. Black probably wanted to prevent White from playing Bg5, but using a move to rule this out smacks of extravagance, especially since Bg5 can be met by the unpinning ...Be7. It's crucial that Black doesn't fall too far behind in development.

7 Bd3

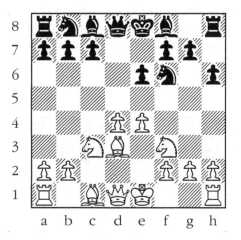

Notice that White is nothing out of the ordinary – just good developing moves.

7...Nc6 8 0-0

Question: Why can't Black grab a pawn with 8...Nxd4 here?

Answer: After 9 Nxd4 Qxd4 White has a decisive discovered attack with 10 Bb5+, winning the black queen.

8...Bd7

Perhaps this is a good time to point out that there's a difference between simply moving pieces and developing them. It's true that Black has just moved the bishop from c8 to d7, but you could hardly call this piece developed. It has no scope and the only square it can move to is back to c8!

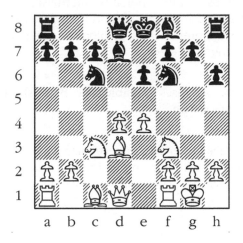

The trouble is that Black is already suffering for his failure to fight for the centre. Black would like to push his e-pawn to e5 so that the light-squared bishop has more freedom, but this is just not possible – all of the crucial central squares are firmly in White's control.

9 Re1

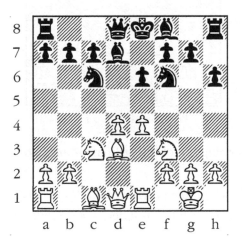

Adding further support to the centre and moving the rook onto the same file as the black king. Black now hurriedly prepares to castle, but unfortunately for him it will be a case of 'out of the frying pan but into the fire'.

9...Bb4 10 a3

Attacking the bishop, which retreats one square.

10...Ba5 11 Bc2!

A clever little retreat, the point of which will be revealed in a few moves.

11...0-0

Black is castling into a storm but it's difficult to suggest anything else.

12 e5!

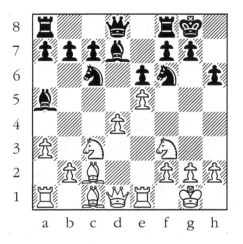

An excellent move, forcing Black to move his defensive knight and opening up the long b1-h7 diagonal for direct attacking purposes. Note how White's bishops point menacingly like trident missiles in the direction of Black's king.

12...Nd5 13 Nxd5!

Now the tactics begin and they unsurprisingly favour White.

13...exd5

If 13...Bxe1 the point of 11 Bc2! is revealed with 14 Qd3!.

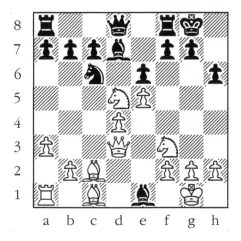

The queen and bishop form a deadly force along the diagonal; the immediate threat is Qh7 mate. Now 14...f5 loses after 15 exf6 when the threat of a devastating Qh7 is still in the air. Instead Black can prevent this with 14...g6 but then White continues with 15 Nf6+! Kg7 16 Nxe1, when White is material ahead and still has a strong attack.

14 b4

Blocking out the threat to the rook on e1 and forcing the bishop to move again.

14...Bb6 15 Qd3!

There are no secrets to White's play; it's simply logical and direct. The threat of Qh7 mate looms again and Black is forced to take evasive action.

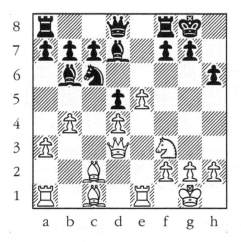

15...g6

This prevents the queen penetrating with devastating effect but there is a price to pay: a vital defensive pawn is lost.

16 Bxh6 Re8

The rook moves out of attack from the bishop. Kasparov now creates a typical checkmating pattern. Black is powerless to prevent this because his king doesn't have enough protection – all his minor pieces are bunched on the queenside.

17 Bg5 Bf5

Black replies to the threat to his queen with a counter-threat to White's.

18 Qd2! Qd7 19 Bf6!

Suddenly Black's in big trouble. White intends to play Qh6, after which Black has no way to deal with the dual threats of Qg7 mate and Qh8 mate.

19...Kh7 20 Qg5

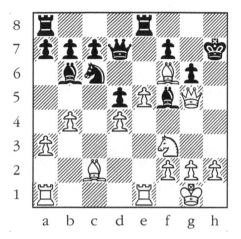

Now White threatens checkmate in two moves with 21 Qh4+ Kg8 22 Qh8 mate.

20...Bg4

To block the check on h4 but...

21 Qh4+ Bh5

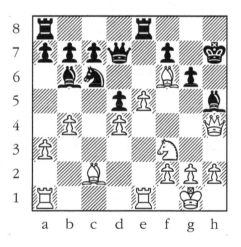

22 Qxh5+! 1-0

The queen is safe because the pawn on g6 is pinned by the bishop on c2. Now Black resigned as it's checkmate next move (22...Kg8 23 Qh8 mate).

The Blocked Centre

So far we've looked at openings where there is either a quick central pawn trade (the Scotch Game; the Open Sicilian) or one where the tension remains in the centre (the Ruy Lopez). However, in some openings the centre very quickly becomes blocked, such as in the French Defence.

1 e4 e6

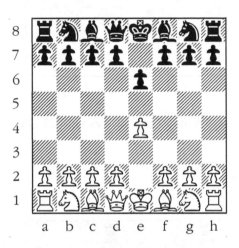

This is certainly a departure from 1...e5 and 1...c5. In the French Defence, Black doesn't actually prevent White from erecting the classical centre. He does, however, create a strongpoint for himself on the d5-square which puts immediate pressure on White's e4-pawn.

2 d4 d5

Okay, White has to do something about Black's simple threat to capture the pawn on e4. Earlier we saw the natural developing move 3 Nc3, and in this chapter we've seen the problem with 3 f3? – 3...dxe4 4 fxe4 Qh4+!. One option for White is to advance the e-pawn, leading to the unsurprisingly named Advance Variation.

3 e5

Now the centre is well and truly blocked. It's easy to see that White has more space than Black and this could become a major advantage: for a start White's development looks as if it will be much easier than Black's.

If Black develops passively there's a very good chance he will get squashed and suffocate. It's imperative that he takes immediate measures to attack and try to destroy White's d4-e5 pawn centre. Assuming White's not going to be foolish enough to leave his d4-pawn en prise to a piece, there is only one strategy for Black to try to dissolve White's centre, and that is using his own pawns. He can attack White's d4-e5 pawn chain at the base with ...c7-c5, at the front with ...f7-f6, or even a combination of both. This type of pawn move is called a pawn break, and we'll look at a few more examples of these throughout the rest of this chapter.

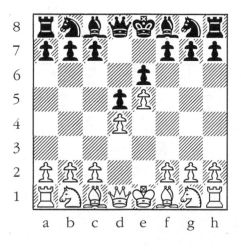

3...c5!

Black begins by attacking the base of White's pawn chain.

4 c3!

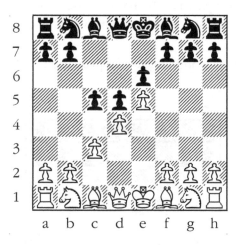

An excellent move, adding further protection to the pawn on d4; in this way it could be said that White is extending the pawn chain. If Black captures on d4 White is ready to recapture with the pawn on c3, thereby keeping a pawn on d4. This is crucial because the pawn on d4 supports White's more advanced pawn on e5.

White should resist the temptation to capture on c5 because this leaves the e5-

pawn weak and White's centre would be in serious danger of crumbling: 4 dxc5?! Nc6! 5 Nf3 Bxc5 (note that Black is already ahead in development) 6 Bd3 and now the consistent way for Black to continue is to eliminate White's only remaining pawn in the centre with 6...f6!, after which White has to be very careful. Defending e5 with 7 Bf4? looks natural, but following 7...fxe5 8 Nxe5? Qf6! White is in real trouble due to the threats on e5, f4 and f2. Instead, after 7 exf6 Nxf6 8 0-0 0-0...

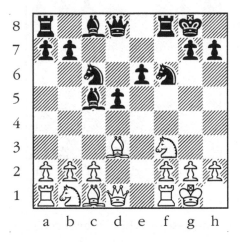

...we see a position where Black's opening strategy has been a success: he is actively developed, White's pawn centre has been destroyed and Black's own pawn centre (e6/d5) is influential and could become very strong.

4...Nc6

Black develops a piece and continues to add pressure to White's centre.

5 Nf3

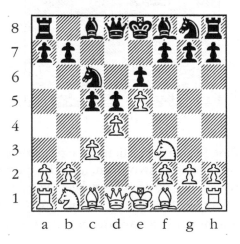

Likewise, White develops and further protects his centre. This is a typical position in the Advance Variation of the French Defence. White has more space but Black is rock-solid. Note that one problem for Black is that the knight on g8 cannot develop on its normal square f6 because this is attacked by the white pawn on e5. Black can get over this problem by playing the knight to e7 (or sometimes even h6) and then to f5 where it plays a major role by further attacking d4.

There are quite a few ways to play for each side from here. Let's just look at one possible line:

5...Qb6

The queen is well placed on b6: it adds mounting pressure to d4 but is far enough back not to become too exposed to attack.

6 Be2

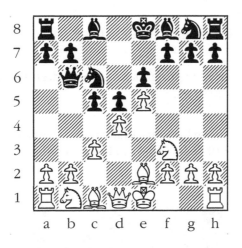

6 Bd3 develops the bishop more actively. Take away five points if you thought Black could now win a pawn with 6...cxd4 7 cxd4 Nxd4?? 8 Nxd4 Qxd4, because White has a decisive discovered attack with 9 Bb5+!. Instead Black should prepare ...Nxd4 with 7...Bd7!, after which defending d4 gives White a headache. Indeed in practice White tends to offer a pawn sacrifice with 8 0-0.

Without wishing to delve into the enormous theory of the Advance French, I would just like to point out that the move 6 a3!? is very popular in tournament play. White both prevents anything coming to b4 and even prepares queenside expansion with b2-b4. Following, say, 6...Nh6 7 b4 cxd4 8 cxd4 Nf5 White can protect the vulnerable d4-pawn with Bb2.

6...cxd4 7 cxd4 Nge7

(see following diagram)

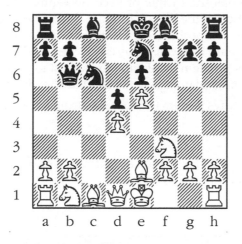

As mentioned earlier, this knight is heading for f5.

8 Na3!?

This knight uses the edge as a springboard: its final destination will be c2 where it will add further protection to d4.

8...Nf5 9 Nc2 Bb4+

Now White is forced to move his king (Black wins a pawn after either 10 Bd2 Bxd2+ 11 Qxd2 Qxb2, or 10 Nxb4 Qxb4+). However, after...

10 Kf1

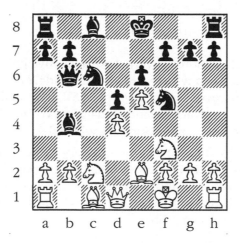

...it's not such a disaster for White that he has lost castling rights: his king is quite safe due to the closed nature of the position. Indeed, White will be able to 'castle by hand' with g2-g3 and Kg2.

Points to remember

1) With the centre blocked play takes on a slower nature. High-speed development isn't quite so important as it is in a more open position.

2) The central pawns shield the kings, making them less vulnerable then in an open position. In view of this there's sometimes not so much of an urgency to castle early.

The Hypermodern School

Up until now we have dealt in the main with the classical way to play chess openings. There are no excuses for this because, after all, most experts agree that newcomers to the game should begin by playing classical openings: it's easier to develop chess skills in this way. However, there is another equally important approach to chess openings which a developing player is especially likely to encounter as he improves. This is called the hypermodern approach, and it advocates speedy development and controlling the centre from a distance with pieces rather than the occupation of the centre with pawns. In many hypermodern openings the opponent is actually invited to occupy the centre with pawns, the idea being that in the long run this centre could be prone to attack.

The hypermodern school of chess came to prominence in the 1920s. Its advocates included two of the leading players of that time: Richard Réti and Aron Nimzowitsch. One of the most popular hypermodern openings around today was the creation of Aron Nimzowitsch and is called the Nimzo-Indian Defence. Let's take a look at one variation of this, which was a big favourite of mine in my youth.

1 d4 Nf6

Even on the first move we see the hypermodernism at work: e2-e4 is prevented by a piece (the knight) rather than a pawn (after 1...d5).

2 c4!

(see following diagram)

As we've seen already in this chapter, the c-pawn plays a vital role in d4 openings. With 2 c4 White is effectively going for 'world domination' in the centre. White now plans to bring the knight out to c3 and follow up with e2-e4.

After 2 Nc3 Black would have no qualms in going back to the classical approach with 2 Nc3 d5!; we saw earlier how difficult it is for White to establish a centre here.

2...e6 3 Nc3

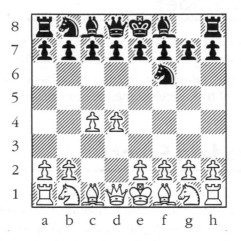

Now White plans e2-e4. Black still has a chance here to revert back to the classical approach with 3...d5, but the hypermodern option is...

3...Bb4!

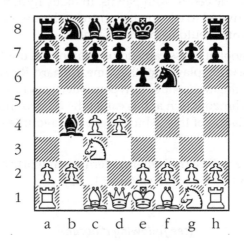

Pinning the knight to the king and thus keeping control of the e4-square: 4 e4? simply loses a pawn to 4...Nxe4!. White now has many different possibilities, but here I will just select one that best illustrates Black's ideas in this line.

4 e3

White decides to develop his kingside with moves such as Bd3 and Nf3. The only small drawback to this move is that the bishop on c1 is temporarily hemmed in. However, 4 e3 is still a very popular response to the Nimzo-Indian.

After 4 e3 Black has a few options, but if Black wishes to continue in hypermodern fashion, the best is probably...

4...b6

This fianchetto really fits in with the hypermodern approach of controlling the centre from a distance. On b7 the bishop plays an active part in the battle for the e4-square.

5 Bd3

White continues to develop classically. Instead 5 Nge2!? may look a little strange as it blocks in the f1-bishop, but this is a playable alternative. White plans to continue with a2-a3 to attack the bishop on b4, and if this is met by ...Bxc3+, White recaptures with the knight on e2.

5...Bb7 6 Nf3

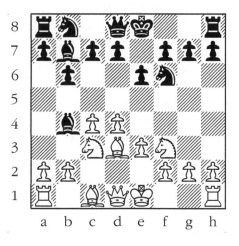

Again White develops in a classical fashion.

6...Ne4!?

This is the most ambitious way for Black to play in this opening system – he continues to control the centre with pieces.

7 Qc2

A natural move, defending the knight on c3 and adding more pressure to e4.

7...f5!

Supporting the knight in the centre and creating possible attacking chances on the kingside (see later).

8 0-0

Now the c3-knight is no longer pinned, so White is threatening to simply win a pawn with Nxe4. Thus Black eliminates this knight before castling.

8...Bxc3 9 bxc3 0-0 10 Nd2

Still the battle for e4 continues, with White taking steps to dislodge the powerful-looking knight. Another way to do this would be with 10 Ne1 and f2-f3.

10...Qh4!

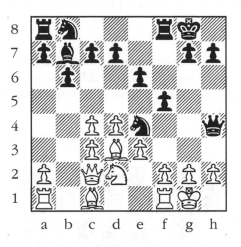

This is an aggressive move that adds extra support to e4 and creates some tactical chances on the kingside. White now has to be very careful – a reason why this system of development is popular amongst Black players.

11 Ba3?

Even though I give this attack on the f8-rooks as the 'main line', 11 Ba3 is actually a big mistake which loses. The notes below indicate White's best course of action.

a) 11 g3?! seems to present problems for Black, as how can the queen stay protecting the knight on e4? Well, the answer is that it doesn't even need to move! Black can play the very cheeky 11...Ng5!!,

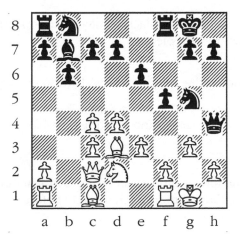

ready to meet 12 gxh4 with 12...Nh3 mate! If White blocks the diagonal with 12 e4 then Black can calmly capture with 12...fxe4! because following 13 gxh4 Nh3+ 14 Kg2 exd3+ 15 Kxh3 dxc2 Black regains the queen with a very good position.

b) 11 f3!, blunting the long diagonal, is White's safest and best move: 11...Nxd2 12 Bxd2 Nc6 13 e4 fxe4 14 fxe4 d6 gives a roughly level position.

11...Nxd2! 12 Qxd2

After 12 Bxf8 the quickest way for Black to win is with 12...Nf3+! 13 gxf3 (or 13 Kh1 Qxh2 mate) 13...Qg5+ 14 Kh1 Bxf3 mate.

12...Bxg2!!

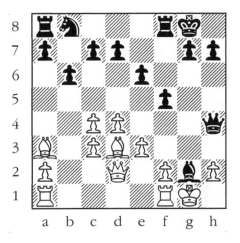

A bolt out of the blue! This sacrifice is a surprisingly common theme and is well worth remembering.

13 Kxg2

If White captures the rook with 13 Bxf8 Black doesn't follow suit with 13...Bxf1 but plays the quiet but devastating 13...Bf3! when White has no way to prevent checkmate, for example 14 Rfc1 Qh3! 15 Bf1 Qg4+ and mate next move.

13...Qg4+ 14 Kh1 Qf3+ 15 Kg1 Rf6!

(see following diagram)

This rook lift onto the third rank reveals another positive point of the earlier move 7...f5. Black did have the option of forcing perpetual check with 15...Qg4+ 16 Kh1 Qf3+ 17 Kg1 Qg4+ etc, but 15...Rf6 aims for much, much more.

16 Rfd1 Qh3!

Very precise play by Black, who now threatens the devastating ...Rg6+. Note that the immediate 16...Rg6+? allows White's king to escape after 17 Kf1.

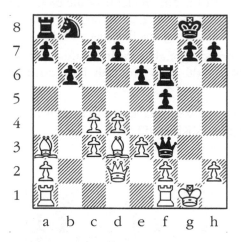

17 f4

There is no defence, for example 17 Bf1 Rg6+ 18 Kh1 Qf3+ 19 Bg2 Qxg2 mate.

17...Rg6+ 18 Kf2 Rg2+

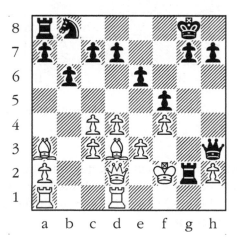

19 Kf1

The only other move was 19 Ke1, but then 19...Rg1+ 20 Kf2 Qg2 is mate.

19...Qf3+ 20 Ke1 Rg1+ 21 Bf1 Rxf1 mate.

Pawn breaks

We've already taken a brief look at a few pawn breaks (1 d4 d5 2 c4!, and 1 e4 e6 2 d4 d5 3 e5 c5! come to mind) but here I'd quite like to look at one or two more. As well as being important weapons in the battle for the centre, pawn breaks are also useful for trying to introduce rooks into the game.

For example, following the opening moves...

1 e4 e5 2 Nf3 Nc6 3 Bb5 a6 4 Ba4 Nf6 5 0-0 b5 6 Bb3 Bc5 7 d3 0-0

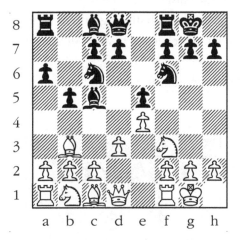

...White has quite a few possibilities (8 Bg5, 8 Be3, 8 Nc3 and 8 c3 all come to mind). Another option, however, is the move...

8 a4!

...the idea being to bring the rook on a1 to life (otherwise it would take a long time for this rook to see any action).

Question: Does White have a threat after 8 a4?

Answer: Yes, simply 9 axb5 is a big threat because Black cannot recapture due to the pin on the a-file.

Black has three main ways of dealing with this problem:

1) He could play 8...Bb7, so that after 9 axb5 axb5 Black's rook is protected

2) He could play 8...Rb8, again so that 9 axb5 can be answered by 9...axb5.

3) He could play 8...b4!?, not allowing the a-file to be opened at all.

Attacking with the f-pawn!

What's this? Just a couple of chapters ago I was harping on about all the problems with moving the f-pawn so early on in the opening. I could imagine you quite rightly demanding 'Make your mind up for goodness sake!' Well, I never said chess was an easy game!

Under the right circumstances (and with due care and attention) the advance of the f-pawn and, in particular, the pawn break with f2-f4 (or ...f5-f7 for Black) can achieve some real positives:

1) It can be useful in the battle for the centre.

2) The f-pawn can be used as a battering ram in an attack.

3) It can be exchanged, which leads to an open file for the rooks.

The following example is a good illustration of how it's possible to activate rooks in the early middlegame.

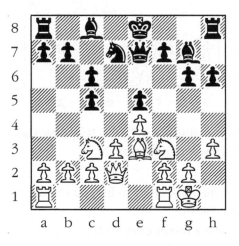

White has all his pieces developed and has castled. The question is what to do next. It would be quite easy here for White to manoeuvre around with his pieces, not really making any progress.

A good question to ask here is, 'How do I activate my rooks?' Here White comes up with a very effective answer.

11 Nh2!

Unblocking the f-pawn.

11...Nf8

The black knight heads for e6, a nice square from where it eyes d4. Note that castling was impossible as the h6-pawn would have been hanging.

12 f4!

Suddenly the rook on f1 is looking a lot happier!

12...exf4 13 Rxf4 Ne6 14 Rf2!

This is better than going all the way back to f1, as White wishes to double rooks on the f-file.

14...Nd4 15 Raf1

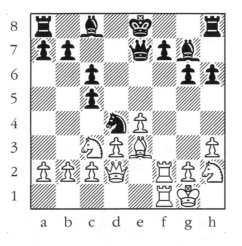

White has made major progress since the previous diagram because now both white rooks are very much in the game.

In some 1 e4 e5 openings White can go for the f2-f4 break very early:

1...e5 2 Bc4

The Bishop's Opening (another name that's easy to work out!). White refrains from playing Nf3 just yet because the f-pawn doesn't want to be blocked.

2...Nf6 3 d3 Nc6 4 Nc3 Be7

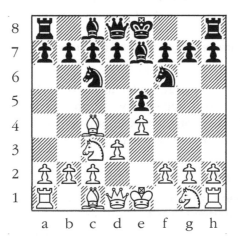

Now White could revert back to 'normality' with 5 Nf3, but much more ambitious is...

5 f4!? d6

...and only now...

6 Nf3

The point is that after White castles kingside his rook immediately finds a role to play along the f-file. From this position let's follow the game G.Mohr-D.Rozakis, Ikaria 1993, which graphically illustrates the attacking chances that White is able to drum up in this type of position.

6...0-0

6...Bg4 is a natural alternative, after which Black may well look to increase the pressure on the pinned knight with ...Nd4. One possible continuation is 7 h3 Bxf3 8 Qxf3 Nd4 and now White can deal with the double attack on f3 and c2 with 9 Qf2.

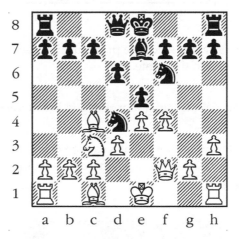

Question: Is 9...Nh5, threatening to win the queen with ...Bh4, a good idea?

Answer: No!

9...Nh5 allows White to demonstrate a tactic based on the opening of the f-file: 10 Bxf7+!! Kxf7 (otherwise the bishop simply captures the knight on h5) 11 fxe5+ (the point: a discovered check leaving the d4-knight en prise) 11...Ke8 12 Qxd4 Bh4+ 13 Kd1 when both kings are no longer able to castle, but it's White who has a healthy extra two pawns.

7 0-0 Bg4 8 Qe1 Qd7 9 f5!

This is another promising way to use the f-pawn. Certainly White could have exchanged on e5 and then tried to use the half-open f-file, but instead here he keeps things closed, the idea being to use the advanced f-pawn as a battering ram for an attack on the kingside. It has to be said that Black is already gasping for air on that side of the board – he is extremely restricted.

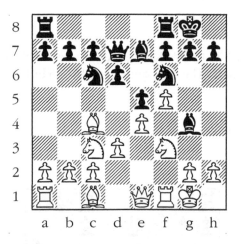

9...Bxf3 10 Rxf3! Nd4 11 Rh3!

White must have seen this idea before agreeing to recapture on f3 with the rook, since defending the c2-pawn with 11 Rf2 would have led to some embarrassment after 11...Ng4!. With 11 Rh3 White is ready to sacrifice a whole rook, and Black doesn't need asking twice.

11...Nxc2 12 Qh4 Nxa1?

Of course this must have been incredibly tempting, but in hindsight Black should have declined the offer, even though White keeps a strong attack after 12...c6 13 Bg5 Rfd8 14 Rf1.

13 Bg5!

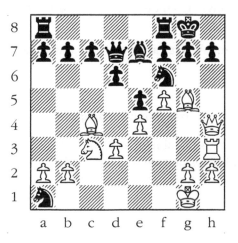

13...c6

Trying desperately to arrange ...d6-d5, but it's too late: White's attack is simply too strong. That said, alternatives are no better at this stage, for example:

a) 13...h6 14 Bxh6! and Black has no chance of survival (14...Nxe4 15 Bg5! and it's mate next move).

b) 13...Rfe8 14 Bxf6 Bxf6 15 Qxh7+ Kf8 16 Nd5!, covering the escape square on e7 and threatening Qh8 mate. The only defence is 16...g6 but after 17 Nxf6 it's all over for Black.

14 Bxf6 h6

The only way to stop Qxh7.

15 Rg3! Bxf6 16 Qxf6 g5

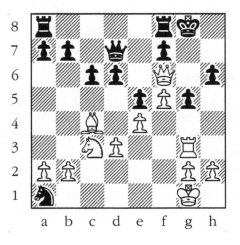

17 Qg6+! 1-0

Using the pin on the f-pawn. It's mate after 17...Kh8 18 Qxh6+ Kg8 19 Rxg5.

Going to the very extreme, White can even try a pawn break with f2-f4 on move two!

1 e4 e5 2 f4!?

(see following diagram)

This is known as the King's Gambit, an opening which is not for the faint-hearted. There are obvious similarities between this and 1 d4 d5 1 c4 (see earlier in the chapter), but in many ways the two openings are worlds apart.

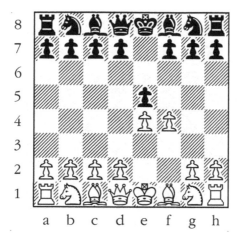

2...exf4

One of the main differences between this and 1 d4 d5 2 c4 is that the King's Gambit is a real gambit: White has no chance of regaining his pawn. If White tries to reclaim his pawn with the idealistic 3 d4, the weakness of White's king is brutally exposed by 3...Qh4+!. White is forced to move his king because 4 g3 fxg3 is disastrous, especially after 5 Nf3 g2+! 6 Nxh4 gxh1Q.

Instead White normally prefers to prevent ...Qh4 with...

3 Nf3

Now Black's most ambitious move here is...

3...g5!

...with the basic idea of holding onto the pawn on f4.

4 Bc4

4 h4!? g4 5 Ne5 Nf6 is another main line. After 4 Bc4 Black can try to consolidate with ...Bg7, ...h7-h6, ...d7-d6 etc, but there's also the enticing alternative of...

4...g4!?

White is reluctant to move his knight on account of ...Qh4+, so instead he adds more fuel to the fire with...

5 0-0!

(see following diagram)

...investing a knight, and there's more to come. This subsection of the King's Gambit is known as the Muzio Gambit, and theory considers the main line to be...

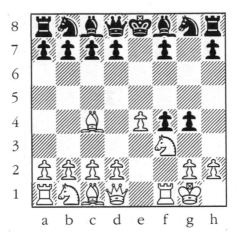

5...gxf3 6 Qxf3 Qf6 7 e5! Qxe5 8 Bxf7+! Kxf7 9 d4 Qxd4+ 10 Be3

...with unfathomable complications. Basically White tries to prove his lead in development and Black's horribly exposed king are more important than the considerable material invested. White either mates Black or dies trying. I repeat: the King's Gambit is not for the faint-hearted!

Understanding Doubled Pawns

Doubled pawns are a tricky subject for inexperienced players to handle. Depending on how much information they've heard, they tend to either ignore the danger completely or else worry too much about the negatives. In fact there are many situations in the opening stages of the game where accepting doubled pawns can be a real benefit. For example:

1 e4 e5 2 Nf3 Nc6 3 Bb5 a6 4 Ba4 Nf6 5 0-0 b5 6 Bb3 Bc5 7 d3

A restrained approach. More aggressive is the typical 7 c3 followed by d2-d4.

7...d6 8 c3 0-0 9 Be3! Bxe3 10 fxe3

There are three things that are worth noticing here:

> 1) With the f-pawn moving from f2 to e3, White now has more control of the centre (on e3 the pawn covers d4 and f4; on f2 it covered only e3).
>
> 2) Even though the e-pawns are doubled, they are not easy to attack.
>
> 3) By playing fxe3 White now has a half-open f-file which can be used as an attacking weapon. Basically, White's rook on f1 has suddenly come to life simply due to this trade on e3.

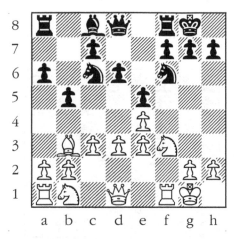

Of course Black isn't forced to capture on e3. Interestingly, he could instead keep the tension, allowing White the opportunity of trading bishops on c5. Let's say Black played a typically useful move in 9...Bg4. Now White could still keep the tension with, say, 10 Nbd2, but there's an obvious temptation to saddle Black with doubled pawns with 10 Bxc5 dxc5.

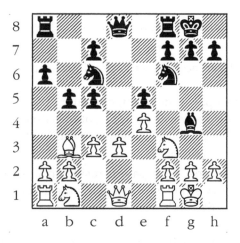

It's true that Black's pawns in the centre (e5 and c5) are slightly more vulnerable now than before the exchange. On the other hand, they perform a good job clamping down on the d4-square. Furthermore, Black now has the opportunity of placing his major pieces on the newly-opened d-file where they will add pressure to White's vulnerable d3-pawn. All in all, not a bad trade for Black.

Strong players are constantly weighing up the pros and cons of accepting or inflicting doubled pawns.

1 e4 e5 2 Nf3 Nc6 3 d4 exd4 4 Nxd4 Nf6 5 Nc3 Bc5 6 Nxc6 bxc6 7 Bd3 d6

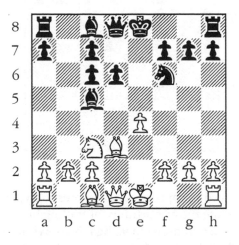

In this position White could play in a similar fashion to the previous example, but here...

8 Be3?

...would be a positional mistake. Following...

8...Bxe3! 9 fxe3

...there are two major differences from the previous example:

> 1) Not only are the e-pawns doubled, crucially they are also isolated – they have no protection from pawns on adjacent files (in the previous example the e4-pawn was handily protected by the one on d3). This means that both e-pawns are long-term weaknesses.
>
> 2) To make matters worse, the e-pawns reside on a half-open file and Black has a very straightforward plan of attacking the e4-pawn with ...0-0, ...Qe7, ...Re8 and perhaps ...Bb7 and ...c6-c5.

It's true that the e-pawns still control some important central squares, and also that White will have some play down the half-open f-file, but there would be real pressure on White to make something of this before his obvious pawn weaknesses really began to tell, and most experienced players would be reluctant to play so riskily.

Going back to White's 8th move, if he were really keen on trading off Black's active bishop on c5, then the right way to go about it would be with...

8 Na4!

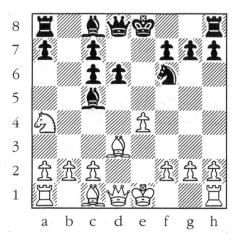

Here it's a case of 'knight on the rim isn't dim' because Black can do nothing to avoid a trade: 8...Bb4+ only prolongs things after 9 c3 Ba5 10 b4! Bb6, while stubbornly avoiding the exchange with 8...Bd4 9 c3 Be5?? only sees the bishop getting trapped after 10 f4!.

Question: Should Black allow a trade on c5 or should he move his bishop to b6?

Answer: Black should play 8...Bb6!.

8...0-0? allows White to inflict not doubled, but tripled pawns with 9 Nxc5! dxc5. Worse for Black, they are also isolated and thus cannot look after themselves. In short, they are permanent weaknesses and Black's open lines do not compensate enough for this.

Following 8...Bb6! 9 Nxb6 Black could 'straighten out' his pawns with 9...cxb6, but actually any grandmaster would instead play 9...axb6!.

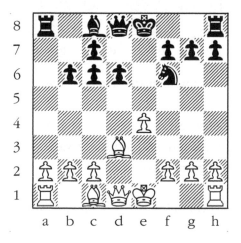

Black's c-pawns are doubled but they certainly couldn't be described as weaknesses. Indeed Black could continue with ...c6-c5 with both a pretty, and pretty effective pawn structure: only the c7-pawn is unprotected here and how is White ever going to attack that? Add to this the sudden activity of Black's rook on a8 and you should begin to see why ...axb6 is preferred to ...cxb6.

A Choice of Pawn Captures

As we have just seen in the previous example, very often a trade of pieces gives a player a choice of pawn recaptures. Deciding which way to recapture can be a tricky business, but considering one or two guidelines can help:

1 e4 c6 2 d4 d5 3 Nc3 dxe4 4 Nxe4 Bf5 5 Ng3 Bg6 6 Nf3 Nd7 7 Bd3 Ngf6

If White now decides to exchange bishops on g6 with...

8 Bxg6

...then Black should definitely reply with

8...hxg6!

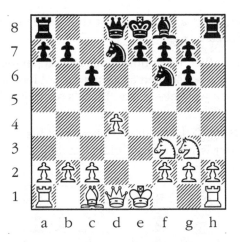

There are three reasons why this is much stronger than 8...fxg6:

    1) Black's pawn structure is much stronger after 8...hxg6 than after 8...fxg6.

    2) Black has more central influence after 8...hxg6.

    3) Black's rook on h8 becomes activated.

An active rook is of course very nice, but as a player's strength increases he begins to appreciate that here this factor is actually less important than the first two reasons given.

Let's look at this a bit deeper. After 8...hxg6 Black has no real pawn weaknesses despite the doubled pawns, which are certainly not vulnerable.

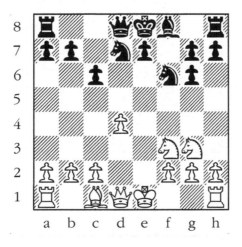

The recapture 8...fxg6, however, suddenly leaves Black with an isolated pawn on e7 and glaringly weak squares on e6 and e5, both of which are potential outposts for White's pieces.

A useful idea in positions like this is to count the number of 'pawn islands' and to implement the guideline 'the fewer the better'. After 8...hxg6 Black has two pawns islands (a7-b7-c6 and e7-f7-g7-g6) while after 8...fxg6 Black has three (a7-b7-c6, e7 and g7-h7-g6).

The other positive of 8...hxg6 is that it gives Black slightly more central control: instead of being on h7, the pawn now resides on g6 and controls f5, while Black keeps the one on f7, controlling e6. With 8...hxg6 Black is doing what's known in the trade as 'capturing towards the centre'.

If in doubt, 'capturing towards the centre' is a very useful guideline to follow. On the other hand, this is certainly not the only consideration. Especially in the early part of the game, ease of development is also crucial. For example:

1 e4 e5 2 Nf3 Nc6 3 Bb5 a6 4 Bxc6

(see following diagram)

Now Black can keep more central pawn control with 4...bxc6, and that is certainly a playable move, but theory considers 4...dxc6 to be stronger because it allows Black easier development (for one things the c8-bishop is ready to move).

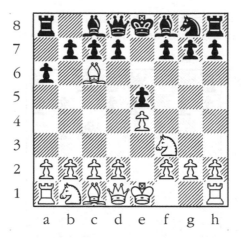

Exercises

1) The Ponziani Opening begins **1 e4 e5 2 Nf3 Nc6 3 c3**. Without delving into any analysis of variations, can you suggest what you think Black's two main moves are here?

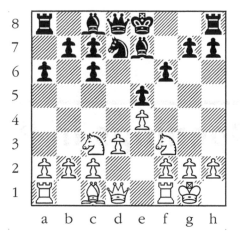

2) This position is reached after the moves **1 e4 e5 2 Nf3 Nc6 3 Bb5 a6 4 Ba4 Nf6 5 0-0 Be7 6 Bxc6 dxc6 7 d3 Nd7 8 Nc3 f6**. Can you suggest an appropriate way forward for White?

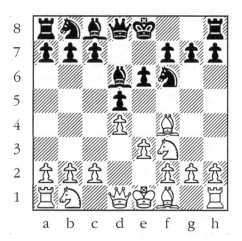

3) This position is reached after **1 d4 d5 2 Nf3 Nf6 3 Bf4 e6 4 e3 Bd6**. If White captures on d6, is it a mistake for Black to recapture with the d-pawn?

Chapter Six

Chess Openings in Practice

In this final chapter it's time to take all the ideas of the previous chapters and see how they help to produce modern opening theory. Given that there have been sets of encyclopaedias spanning well over a thousand pages devoted solely to existing chess openings (and even then without any verbal commentary!), I can't hope to be anywhere near comprehensive here. But then again that was never the point of this book. Opening theory is a never-ending maze of variations and sub-variations; the further you delve, the more complex it gets – it's difficult to know where to stop. I've limited myself to looking at a selection of 'main lines' in popular openings that haven't been covered elsewhere in this book, indulging in one or two I believe an improving player is more likely to come across as either White or Black, and giving a bit more detail to the overly tactical lines.

If you find an opening here that appeals to you and you wish to find out more about it, the next step would be to obtain an introductory text devoted entirely to that subject. For this purpose I can happily recommend Everyman Chess's *Starting Out* series, which specializes in opening books for improving players.

The Giuoco Piano

1 e4 e5 2 Nf3 Nc6 3 Bc4

(see following diagram)

We've already come across the Giuoco Piano a few times in this book. Here I'll go over one or two lines that we haven't covered so far.

3...Bc5

This is a very sensible move; Black simply reacts in a similar fashion to White. 3...Nf6 will be covered a bit later.

4 c3

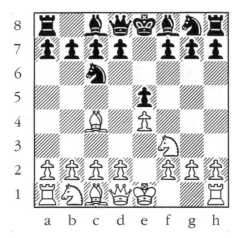

This is possibly White's most logical move. With 4 c3 he is preparing to build the classical centre with d2-d4. This plan looks especially appealing given that d4 will gain time by attacking the c5-bishop.

The Evans Gambit (4 b4) and the quiet 4 d3 were covered in Chapter 4.

4...Nf6!

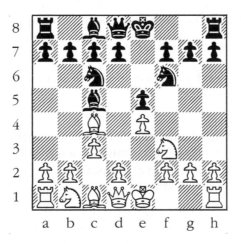

We've seen this concept a few times now: Black counterattacks by threatening the pawn on e4 and reveals the only negative feature of 4 c3: White's knight on b1 no longer has access to the c3-square.

4...d6!? is certainly playable, although it does allow White to carry out his plan: 5 d4! exd4 (Black is forced to give up the centre because of the tactic 5...Bb6 6 dxe5! Nxe5 – or 6...dxe5 7 Qxd8+ Nxd8 8 Nxe5 – 7 Nxe5 dxe5 8 Bxf7+!) 6 cxd4 Bb6 7 Nc3 Nf6 8 d5 Ne5 9 Nxe5 dxe5 10 Bg5 with a slight advantage for White.

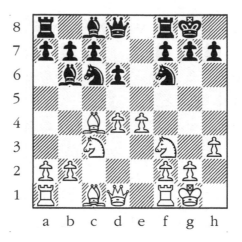

Question: After 8 h3 (preventing ...Bg4) 8...0-0 9 0-0 (see the diagram above) can you see a good move for Black?

Answer: 9...Nxe4! 10 Nxe4 d5! completely breaks up White's centre. This is a very useful trick to remember.

5 d4

The move most consistent with 4 c3. White can also play more slowly with 5 d3, defending e4. With this quiet move White doesn't give up on the idea of d4 completely; he wants to play it at a stage where he is fully developed.

5...exd4

More or less forced. Hopefully you should realize by now that 5...Bd6?, blocking the d-pawn, is a poor move.

6 cxd4

This recapture is almost automatic, but it's always worth hesitating just for a moment and asking yourself if there's a worthwhile alternative. In fact White does have a significant option here in the very logical 6 e5!?, gaining time by attacking the knight before recapturing on d4.

If Black were forced to move the knight then he would begin to suffer, for example 6...Ng4 7 cxd4 Bb4+ 8 Nc3 followed by h2-h3, sidelining the knight; or 6...Ne4 7 Bd5! f5 8 cxd4 Bb4+ 9 Nbd2 and Black cannot castle. Crucially for Black, he can play the move 6...d5!...

(see following diagram)

...and following the exchanges 7 exf6 dxc4 8 fxg7 Rg8 9 cxd4 Nxd4 10 0-0 Qf6! Black has nothing to fear, despite his kingside being wrecked and his king being in the middle. Black will block the e-file with ...Be6 and follow up with ...0-0-0.

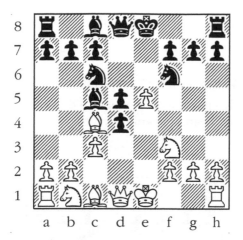

Instead of 7 exf6, White can play 7 Bb5! Ne4 8 cxd4 after which both 8...Bb4+ and 8...Bb6 lead to a roughly equal position.

This idea of answering the e4-e5 threat with the ...d7-d5 counter-threat is well worth remembering as it crops up quite a few times in 1 e4 e5 openings.

6...Bb4+!

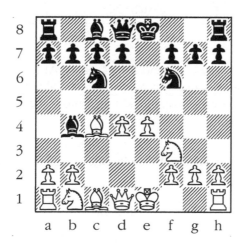

Another good move: Blacks gains time by giving a check. Now we will look at:

A: 7 Bd2

B: 7 Nc3!?

A)

1 e4 e5 2 Nf3 Nc6 3 Bc4 Bc5 4 c3 Nf6 5 d4 exd4 6 cxd4 Bb4+ 7 Bd2

The safest move.

7...Bxd2+

Question: What does White play after 7...Nxe4 here?

Answer: White regains his pawn with the tactic 8 Bxb4 Nxb4 9 Bxf7+! Kxf7 10 Qb3+, forking the king on f7 and the knight on b4.

8 Nbxd2

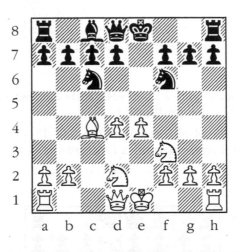

White must capture this way to defend the e4-pawn. At first sight it looks like White's opening has been a great success: he has developed most of his pieces and possesses the classical pawn centre. Black's next move, however, assures him of a fair share of the chances.

8...d5!

Striking back in the centre – one of White's pawns will be eliminated.

9 exd5 Nxd5 10 Qb3!

(see following diagram)

This is the move that causes Black most problems. The knight is attacked and moving it allows Bxf7+, while the most natural defence, 10...Be6, leaves the b7-pawn en prise.

10...Nce7

10...Na5!? is an unusual solution to Black's problems; unusual in that after the obvious 11 Qa4+ Black's intention is not 11...c6 (after which 12 Bxd5! Qxd5 13 Rc1 threatening Rc5 is uncomfortable) but instead the retreat 11...Nc6!. It seems that apart from offering a repetition of moves with 12 Qb3, White cannot exploit Black's little knight dance: 12 Bb5 Bd7 13 0-0 0-0 looks roughly equal.

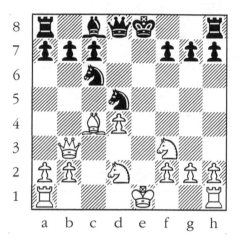

11 0-0 0-0 12 Rfe1 c6

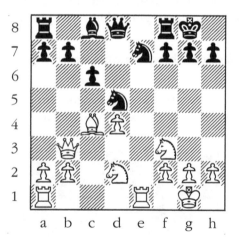

Both sides have developed comfortably. White has a bit more activity but Black is incredibly solid; all in all, fairly equal.

B)

1 e4 e5 2 Nf3 Nc6 3 Bc4 Bc5 4 c3 Nf6 5 d4 exd4 6 cxd4 Bb4+ 7 Nc3!?

This is much more aggressive than 7 Bd2. White is prepared to sacrifice at least one pawn for the cause of rapid development. In the final analysis 7 Nc3 (known as the Møller Attack) is probably not quite sound, but that doesn't prevent numerous tournament players trying their luck with it.

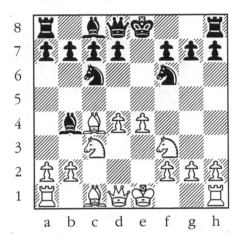

7...Nxe4!

If Black is unwilling to enter the complications then 7...d5 is a playable alternative, which was covered in Chapter 3. However, Steinitz's assertion that 'the refutation of a gambit frequently lies in its acceptance' is very apt here.

8 0-0!

Continuing in gambit fashion. There is simply no time to defend c3.

8...Bxc3!

The problems Black faces if he plays any sort of inaccuracy are graphically illustrated in the following variations: 8...Nxc3?! 9 bxc3 Bxc3? (9...d5!) 10 Ba3!...

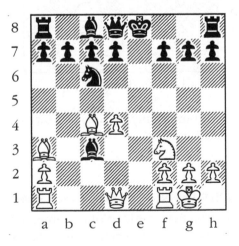

...and Black, with is king stuck uncomfortably in the centre, is in real trouble. For example:

a) 10...Bxa1 11 Re1+! and White wins immediately.

b) 10...d6 11 Rc1! Ba5 12 Qa4 (threatening d4-d5) 12...a6 13 Bd5! Bb6 14 Rxc6! Bd7 (14...bxc6 15 Bxc6+ Bd7 16 Re1+ Kf8 17 Bxd7) 15 Re1+ Kf8 16 Rxd6!! cxd6 17 Bxd6+ Kg8 18 Qb3! and White's attack is crushing.

c) 10...d5 11 Bb5! Bxa1 12 Re1+! Be6 13 Qa4! Rc8 14 Ne5 and again it's unlikely that Black will survive the onslaught.

It's lines such as these that unsurprisingly entice players into trying out the move 7 Nc3.

Getting back to 8...Bxc3, now the pedestrian 9 bxc3 is answered by 9...d5! followed by kingside castling, after which White really has no compensation for the pawn deficit. Because of this, White normally complicates matters even further with...

9 d5!

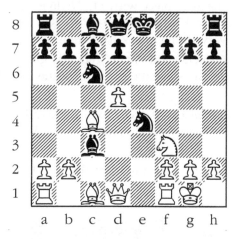

Black is still a piece (not to mention the pawn) ahead but now has two pieces attacked.

9...Bf6

Safeguarding one of the threatened pieces, but in such a complex position it's unsurprising that Black has alternatives here:

a) It's obviously tempting to rush the king into safety with 9...0-0 but White's initiative remains after 10 bxc3, for example 10...Ne7 11 Re1 Nf6 12 Bg5! Ng6 and now the constraining 13 d6! looks good.

b) 9...Ne5 is a solid option: 10 bxc3! Nxc4 11 Qd4...

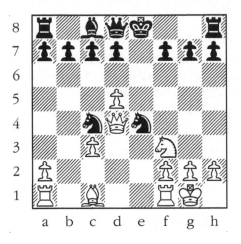

...and now:

b1) Trying to hold onto the extra piece with 11...Ncd6 is risky after 12 Qxg7, e.g. 12...Qf6? (12...Rf8 is stronger) 13 Qxf6 Nxf6 14 Re1+ Kf8 15 Bh6+ Kg8 16 Re5! Nfe4 17 Re1 f6 18 Re7 with a very strong attack for White.

b2) 11...0-0! 12 Qxe4 Nd6 13 Qd3 and White's activity gives some compensation, but Black is very solid and can solve the problem of the c8-bishop with 13...b6!.

10 Re1!

The right way to regain the piece. 10 dxc6? bxc6 solves all Black's problems, as after 11 Re1 d5 he is ready to castle and White is struggling to find compensation.

10...Ne7 11 Rxe4 d6!

A crucial move. Once more it's tempting to castle, but 11...0-0 12 d6! clogs up Black's development.

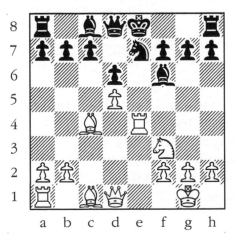

After 11...d6 Black has consolidated somewhat and is still a pawn ahead, but White still has some initiative. Let's look a bit further:

12 Bg5! Bxg5 13 Nxg5 h6!?

13...0-0 14 Nxh7!? Kxh7 15 Qh5+ Kg8 16 Rh4 is incredibly complex and has apparently been worked out to lead to a perpetual check!

14 Qe2!

This pseudo piece sacrifice is the only real way to keep things going. After 14 Nf3 Black can finally heave a sigh of relief and castle into safety.

14...hxg5 15 Re1

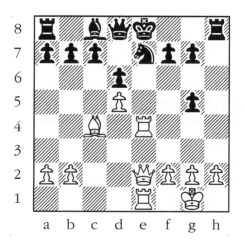

By tripling on the e-file White is assured of regaining the piece. Things look grim for Black but...

15...Be6!!

An imaginative way of blocking White's major route of attack, the e-file.

After the plausible 15...0-0? 16 Rxe7 White's attack is assuming very dangerous proportions, e.g. 16...Bf5 17 Qh5! when 17...f6? is met by the delightful idea of 18 Bb5! intending Be8! followed by Bf7+. I don't actually see a defence to this plan.

16 dxe6 f6

A very unclear position has arisen. At first sight Black, behind in development and with a huge pawn on e6 to contend with, looks in some trouble, but a closer look reveals that it's actually hard for White to make progress because of the blocked nature of the position. Black's position is quite solid: he still has that extra pawn and plans ...c7-c6, moving the queen and castling queenside. 17 Re3 planning Rh3 to exchange rooks and thus give the queen access to h5, is possibly the line that gives Black most to think about.

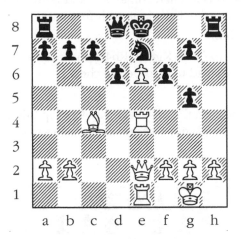

The Two Knights Defence

1 e4 e5 2 Nf3 Nc6 3 Bc4 Nf6

This is known as the Two Knights Defence (for obvious reasons). Despite being a logical developing move, 3...Nf6 is seen as more risky than 3...Bc5 because it allows White the enticing possibility of...

4 Ng5!?

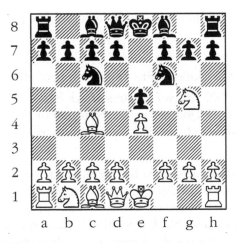

...attacking the f7-pawn. Black is virtually forced to sacrifice a pawn after 4 Ng5. There are many hair-raising variations, but here I'll restrict myself to the one considered by most to be the main line.

If White is looking for sharp, gambit play where it is he and not Black who gives up a pawn, then opening up the position with 4 d4 is the obvious choice. Those looking for quieter paths will prefer 4 d3. The move 4 Nc3 also defends e4, but this allows Black the outwardly surprising idea of 4...Nxe4!, the point being that after 5 Nxe4 Black regains the piece with the fork 5...d5! and reaches a very comfortable position. Instead, the desperado 5 Bxf7+ Kxf7 6 Nxe4 at first sight looks nice for White due to Black's open king, but following 6...d5 7 Neg5+ Kg8...

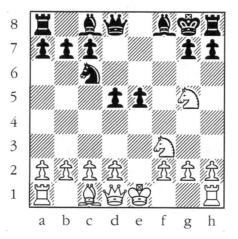

...Black's ideal pawn centre and White's awkwardly placed knights more than make up for this, e.g. 8 d3 h6! 9 Nh3 Bg4! (threatening ...Nd4) 10 c3 Qf6 and I would prefer to have Black's position.

This ...Nxe4 trick is useful to remember, as it crops up in more than one opening.

4...d5

The only move? Actually, no! Those with a penchant for crazy, attacking chess would have fun investigating 4...Bc5!?, the Traxler Variation. Black's idea is to meet 5 Nxf7 with 5...Bxf2+! after which you reach positions that are best analysed with the help of a powerful computer engine!

5 exd5 Na5

The whole point behind 4 Ng5 is that the natural recapture 5...Nxd5 is extremely risky as Black has tactical problems with his f7-pawn, e.g. 6 d4! exd4? 7 0-0! Be6 8 Re1 Qd7

(see following diagram)

9 Nxf7!! (an amazing sacrifice) 9...Kxf7 (9...Bxf7 is illegal due to the pin on the e-file, while 9...Qxf7 is answered by 10 Bxd5!) 10 Qf3+ Kg6? (10...Kg8 is better, but White is still doing well after 11 Rxe6!) 11 Rxe6+ Qxe6 12 Bd3+ Qf5 13 Qxf5 mate.

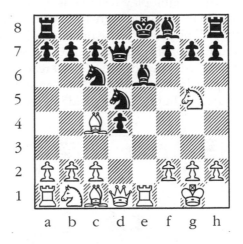

6 Bb5+ c6 7 dxc6 bxc6 8 Be2!

8 Ba4 looks more natural, but the unprotected bishop on a4 gives Black a crucial tactical possibility: 8...h6! 9 Nf3 e4! 10 Ne5 Qd4 when the double attack wins a piece (after 11 Bxc6+ Nxc6 12 Nxc6 Qd5 the knight is trapped).

8...h6

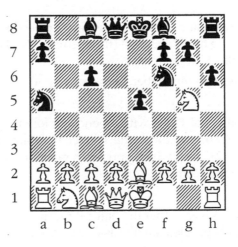

Black's compensation for the pawn only materializes if he harasses this knight before White has a chance to consolidate. For this reason, something like the plausible 8...Bc5 is less accurate: 9 Nc3! and now 9...h6 can be met by 10 Nge4!.

9 Nf3 e4!

And again, before White can play d2-d3.

10 Ne5 Bd6

Once more!

11 d4 exd3 12 Nxd3 Qc7!

Another important move, preventing White from castling just yet due to the attack on h2.

13 h3 0-0 14 0-0 c5

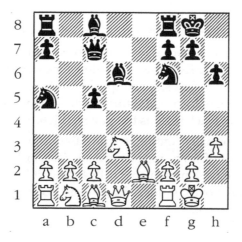

Black's slight lead in development and more active pieces give him more or less sufficient compensation for the pawn.

The Ruy Lopez

1 e4 e5 2 Nf3 Nc6 3 Bb5

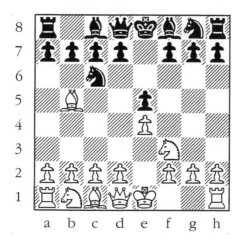

We've already looked at some ideas and a few lines of the Ruy Lopez (it's also known as the Spanish Opening) earlier on in the book. Here I'd just like to fill in one or two gaps in the main line.

3...a6

Immediately putting the question to the bishop on b5 is Black's most popular response, but developing moves such as 3...Nf6 and 3...Bc5 are also sensible.

4 Ba4

The bishop retreats from the attack, but still keeps the pressure on the c6-knight.

It's also possible, of course, to exchange bishop for knight with 4 Bxc6 dxc6 – this is unimaginatively called the Exchange Variation. One important point to note here is that 5 Nxe5, which at first sight simply seems to win a pawn for nothing, can be answered favourably by 5...Qd4! forking the knight on e5 and the pawn on e4. Following, say, 6 Nf3 Black regains the pawn with 6...Qxe4+.

Because of this White normally continues with 5 0-0!, after which Black can protect the e5-pawn in a number of ways, including 5...f6, 5...Bd6, 5...Qd6 (preparing queenside castling) or, most ambitiously, 5...Bg4. Now if White attacks the bishop with 6 h3 then the main move considered by theory is neither 6...Bh5 nor 6...Bxf3 but the surprising idea 6...h5!.

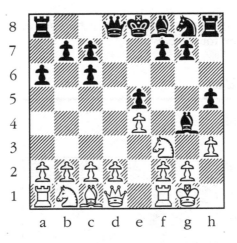

White does well to resist the temptation of capturing the bishop and instead be content with 7 d3!, because after 7 hxg4?! hxg4 the h-file is opened and White is forced to return his piece advantage immediately. Refusing to do so leads to a catastrophe: 8 Nxe5?? Qh4! 9 f4 g3! and there is nothing White can do to avoid ...Qh1 mate!

Going back to fifth move alternatives, note here that I didn't criticize the move 5...f6. Though not ideal in certain respects (the knight no longer has its favourite square), here it doesn't endanger Black's king because:

1) White has traded his already light-squared bishop (no more Bc4 to worry about).

2) Black will quickly castle queenside, so the weakness on the kingside caused by ...f6 is less of a problem.

Remember: guidelines are guidelines, not rules!

4...Nf6

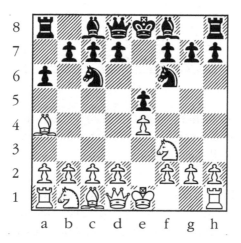

Good, sensible opening play, developing the knight and attacking the e4-pawn.

5 0-0

Ignoring the 'threat' to the e4-pawn.

5...Be7

The safest move: Black develops the bishop to a solid, defensive position and prepares to castle.

We've already looked at 5...b5 in Chapters 4 and 5. The other main line is to grab on e4 with 5...Nxe4 and now White usually plays 6 d4, trying to blast open the centre to expose Black's king. Black's most sensible approach is to give back the pawn via 6...b5 7 Bb3 d5! 8 dxe5 Be6 – this is known as the Open Ruy Lopez.

6 Re1

We saw this idea in the previous chapter. White uses the rook to protect the e4-pawn and is now ready to expand in the centre with c2-c3 followed by d2-d4.

6...b5

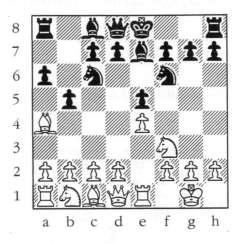

Given that White had protected his pawn on e4, he was threatening to win a pawn himself with 7 Bxc6 dxc6 8 Nxe5, so Black blocks the attack on c6 thus preventing an exchange of pieces on that square.

7 Bb3 d6

Giving the e5-pawn added protection and preparing to develop the bishop on c8.

More ambitious is 7...0-0, planning to cut across White's main plan after 8 c3 with 8...d5!? – this is known as the Marshall Gambit. After 9 exd5 Nxd5 10 Nxe5 Nxe5 11 Rxe5 White wins a pawn, but following, say, 11...c6 12 d4 Bd6 13 Re1 Qh4 14 g3 Qh3...

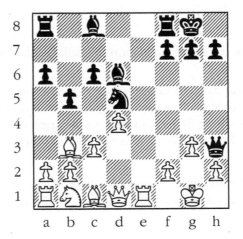

...Black has the initiative and long-term chances on the kingside. The Marshall Gambit is well respected, even at the highest levels, so much so that many grandmasters refuse to allow Black the possibility, instead preferring moves such as 8 a4, 8 d3 and 8 h3.

8 c3 0-0

Finally Black's king moves into safety.

9 h3

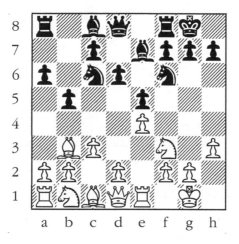

The final preparation for the move d2-d4: White avoids what could have been an annoying pin with ...Bg4. That said 9 d4 is also fully playable, with White meeting 9 ...Bg4 with either 10 Be3 or 10 d5. After 9 h3 the stage is set for a complex middlegame in which both sides have reasonable chances, but typically with White holding a theoretical edge.

The Petroff Defence

It would be inappropriate if I went through the whole of this book leading you to believe that Black has to defend the e-pawn after...

1 e4 e5 2 Nf3

In fact, Black has an equally playable move in...

2...Nf6

(see following diagram)

...answering the threat to e5 with a counter-threat to e4.

3 Nxe5

If Black wishes to play like this, one thing he must learn straight away is that 3...Nxe4? can lead to a catastrophe down the e-file after 4 Qe2! Nf6 5 Nc6+ when the discovered check nets Black's queen. Black can avoid a total disaster with 4...Qe7 5 Qxe4 d6!, exploiting the pin, but will remain a pawn down after 6 d4.

Instead of 3...Nxe4? Black should play the zwischenzug...

3...d6!

...when play usually continues...

4 Nf3 Nxe4

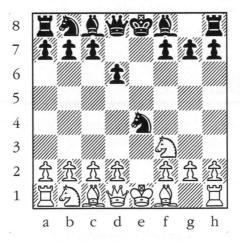

Now 5 Qe2 can be safely answered by 5...Qe7! and following 6 d3 Nf6 an early queen trade is likely. White tends to play more ambitiously with...

5 d4 d5 6 Bd3

...when there are a number of ways for Black to continue (6...Nc6, 6...Be7, 6...Bd6) but it's easy to see that he basically has a sound position. White castles and then usually goes for the pawn break c2-c4, trying to destabilize Black's knight in the centre. One of the main lines runs 6...Bd6 7 0-0 0-0 8 c4 c6 9 cxd5 cxd5 10 Nc3 Nxc3 11 bxc3.

The Sicilian Dragon

1 e4 c5 2 Nf3

In Chapter 5 we looked at one or two lines after 2 c3. Alternatives for White include 2 Nc3 followed by g2-g3 (the Closed Sicilian), 2 f4 (the Grand Prix Attack) and the gambits 2 d4 cxd4 3 c3 (the Morra Gambit) and 2 b4 (the Wing Gambit).

2...d6

So that Black can play ...Nf6 without having to worry about e4-e5.

3 d4

Opting for the Open Sicilian. 3 Bb5+ is a most logical alternative (see Chapter 5).

3...cxd4 4 Nxd4 Nf6 5 Nc3

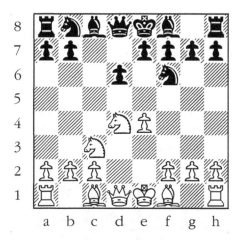

This is a typical starting point in the Open Sicilian, after which Black has quite a few options (5...Nc6, 5...e6, 5...a6). Here I will just look briefly at one possibility, the so-called Dragon Variation, which was one of the first openings I learned as a junior.

5...g6

The Dragon Variation is the Sicilian in its most natural and logical form. Black develops his pieces on their most active squares. In particular, the 'Dragon bishop' is fianchettoed on the long diagonal, down which it exerts its significant presence.

6 Be3

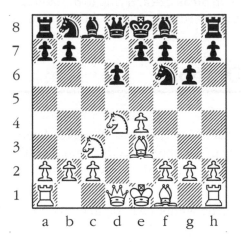

A normal developing move, but White is already thinking well into the future. Theory considers White's most dangerous plan is to quickly develop his queen-side, castle long and then turn his attention to an all-out assault on Black's king.

6...Bg7

Attacking the bishop with 6...Ng4?? is a bad mistake as the reply 7 Bb5+! wins material after either 7...Nc6 8 Nxc6 bxc6 9 Bxc6+ Bd7 10 Bxa8 or 7...Bd7 8 Qxg4 (the bishop on d7 is pinned).

7 f3

Preventing ...Ng4 and thus preparing Qd2 and 0-0-0. One of White's main ideas is to play Bh6, forcing the exchange of Black's main defensive piece on the kingside.

7...Nc6 8 Qd2 0-0 9 Bc4 Bd7 10 0-0-0

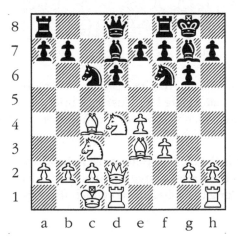

The 'starting position' of the main line of the Dragon. With opposite-side castling exciting play is in prospect, with both players attacking their opponent's king. Very briefly, here's what's going on.

White plans the following:

1) Prise open the h-file with h2-h4-h5, perhaps supported by g2-g4.

2) Exchange off Black's main defenders on the kingside. The Dragon bishop on g7 can be exchanged with Bh6. The defensive knight on f6 can be exchange or eliminated in a number of ways, including Nd5 and g4-g5.

3) In the words of Bobby Fischer, 'pry open the h-file, sac, sac ...mate!'

Black plans to gain counterplay on the queenside, with moves such as ...Ra8-c8, ...Ne5-c5, ...b7-b5 and ...Qd8-a5. Sometimes Black sacrifices a rook for knight with ...Rc8xc3, disrupting the pawn structure around the White king. Defensively, Black can consider halting the advance of White's h-pawn with ...h7-h5. Although this allows White to continue an attack with g2-g4, this is sometimes more diffi-cult to arrange. If given time, Black may move the f8-rook, a point of which is to answer Bh6 with ...Bh8, keeping the Dragon bishop, which performs such a good job along the long diagonal both in defence and attack.

The Sicilian Sveshnikov

1 e4 c5 2 Nf3 Nc6

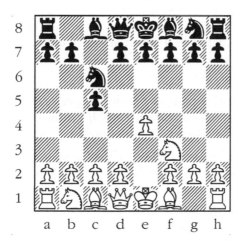

3 d4

The main alternative for White here is to play in Ruy Lopez fashion with 3 Bb5, although if Black plays 3...a6 White should certainly capture on c6, as 4 Ba4?? b5! 5 Bb3 c4 would be embarrassing!

3...cxd4 4 Nxd4 Nf6 5 Nc3

More than one person has fallen for 5 Nxc6 bxc6 6 e5? when 6...Qa5+! picks up the e5-pawn.

5...e5

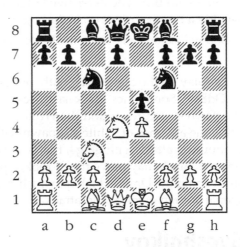

Typical opening play: Black gains by developing and attacking an enemy piece. On a fundamental level, the Sveshnikov is the most ambitious variation of the Sicilian, with Black immediately looking to put his extra central pawn to good use. If White doesn't know what he is doing, it's incredibly easy for him to wind up in an inferior position. On the other hand, Black is accepting a major weakness here in the d5-square. In the main line this is truly in White's possession and is used as an enticing outpost for the c3-knight.

6 Ndb5!

This is considered by most experts as the only move that gives White a chance of fighting for some kind of opening advantage. If White simply retreats his knight, Black develops quickly with threats. For example:

a) 6 Nb3 Bb4! when 7 Bd3 can be met with 7...d5!; or similarly 6 Nf3 Bb4!. White can avoid losing time with the trade 6 Nxc6, but Black can be very happy after 6...bxc6!: his centre is strengthened and his rook can gain activity with ...Rb8.

b) 6 Nf5 is a tempting move with similar motives to 6 Nb5 (the idea of Nd6+), but Black can gain an equal position if he plays the energetic 6...d5 utilizing the idea of ...Bxf5, e.g. 7 exd5 Bxf5 8 dxc6 bxc6.

Going back to 6 Nbd5, the real strength of this move is that Black doesn't really want to allow the check on d6, e.g. 6...a6 7 Nd6+! Bxd6 8 Qxd6 Qe7 9 Qxe7+ Kxe7 10 Bg5! and I like White here. Because of this, Black feels obliged to play...

6...d6

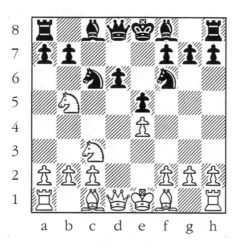

...but now Black's bishop on f8 doesn't enjoy the freedom of being able to play ...Bb4 or ...Bc5. So 6 Ndb5 is a necessary piece of restrictive play by White, but it does come at a cost: the knight on b5 is in serious danger of being sidelined.

7 Bg5!

Working through the Sveshnikov with some junior students who had no knowledge of the theory, it was interesting to see that they really liked the move 7 Nd5 and initially assessed it as clearly better for White. Due to the horrific threat of Nc7+, Black really has no choice but to trade on d5. Following 7...Nxd5 8 exd5 Nb8 (theory prefers this to 8...Ne7)

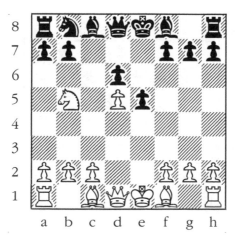

it is easy to see why White's position might appeal at first sight: he has more space and the knight on b5 looks threatening. However, Black will soon force the knight away with ...a7-a6, while the d6-e5 central pawn duo gives his position a very solid feel (he'll follow up with ...Be7 and ...0-0 before perhaps expanding on the kingside with ...f7-f5). In truth, the position is roughly level.

7...a6!

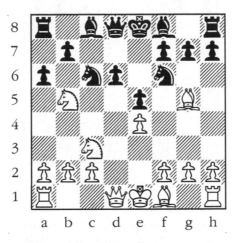

8 Na3

After 8 Bxf6 of course Black must recapture with the pawn as 8...Qxf6?? allows the fork 9 Nc7+. But those wishing to play the Sveshnikov soon realize that this pawn recapture is par for the course, and following 8...gxf6 9 Na3 Black can immediately both eliminate his doubled pawn and fight for control of the central squares with the pawn break 9...f5!.

8...b5!

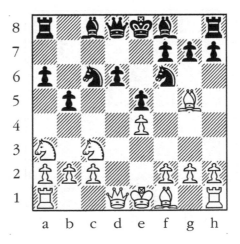

Completely sidelining White's a3-knight (Nc4 is no longer possible), making it the worst placed minor piece on the board, even though White has spent four of his first eight moves on this piece. Normally such extravagance would be suicidal, but in return White has managed to induce Black into accepting some glaring weaknesses, none more so than the big hole on d5.

This is the main starting point of the Sveshnikov, which now spirals into a huge mass of complex theory. White has to deal with the threat of ...b5-b4 and this he does with either 9 Nd5 or 9 Bxf6 followed by 10 Nd5. After 9 Bxf6 the first thought of many a player would be the automatic recapture 9...Qxf6. However, time is of the essence here, and White probably gains too much of it after 10 Nd5 (I won't attempt to explain the complexities here; a good book entirely devoted to the Sveshnikov is what's required). So instead Black opts for 9...gxf6 and after 10 Nd5 Black usually plays 10...f5 and then the fun begins...

The French

1 e4 e6 2 d4 d5

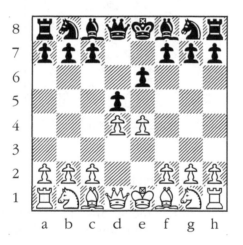

We've already looked at a couple of lines of the French Defence in Chapters 2 and 5, so here I'm just filling in one or two gaps.

3 Nc3

Defending the e-pawn in the most natural way is considered the main move by theory. In Chapter 5 we saw White opting to immediately block the centre with the space-gaining e4-e5, while there are two other possibilities that are worth mentioning:

a) The most simplistic way for White to deal with the threat to the e4-pawn is with

3 exd5 (the Exchange Variation). Black should now recapture with 3...exd5! giving him just as much presence in the centre as White and also opening the way for the c8-bishop to develop (given it's usually blocked by the pawn on e6, finding activity for this piece is one of Black's major tasks in the French).

b) The advantage 3 Nd2 has over 3 Nc3 is that it pretty much avoids the possibility of the bishop pin (3...Bb4?! achieves nothing as White can simply break the pin and chase the bishop with 4 c3!). On the other hand, on d2 the knight is certainly not as actively placed and of course it blocks the c1-bishop. One major continuation for Black is 3...Nf6 and following the logical 4 e5 Nfd7 play resembles that seen in the Advance Variation (4...Ne4 is also possible but Black must be wary that after 5 Nxe4 dxe4 the e4-pawn could become vulnerable).

Given the slight awkwardness of 3 Nd2, there's a strong temptation for Black to strike in the centre with 3...c5 and indeed this is Black's most popular response.

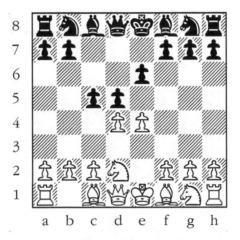

Now White chooses between releasing the tension with 4 exd5 when both 4...exd5 and 4...Qxd5 (there's no Nc3!) are played, or keeping the tension with 4 Ngf3. This tension could remain for one or two moves after 4...Nc6 5 Bb5, or Black could choose to trade with 4...cxd4 5 Nxd4 and now 5...Nc6, planning to meet 6 Bb5 with 6...Bd7.

3...Bb4

The Winawer Variation, Black's most ambitious way to play the position after 3 Nc3. The threat to e4 is renewed and this pin on the c3-knight can prove to be awkward for White.

We briefly looked at 3...dxe4 4 Nxe4 in Chapter 2. Releasing the tension gives White the edge in the centre: the structure of d4 versus e6 gives White more space and easier development. On the other hand, just as in many lines of the French, Black keeps a rock-solid position, and he will aim to nibble at White's d-pawn in the near future with the pawn break ...c7-c5.

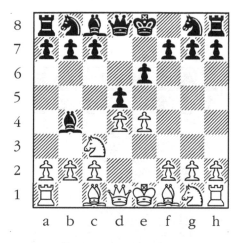

Black's main alternative to 3...Bb4 is 3...Nf6 which usually encourages White to block the centre with a gain of tempo after 4 e5 (or the similar 4 Bg5 Be7 5 e5 Nfd7).

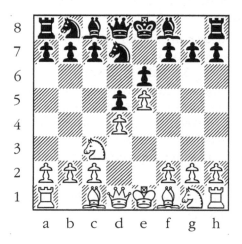

Taking the position after 4 e5 Nfd7, there's again obvious similarities with the Advance Variation. What's worth realizing here, though, is that given White likes to answer the pawn break ...c7-c5 with c2-c3, his knight on c3 isn't ideally placed. One way to prepare for the ...c5 lunge is with 5 Nce2!?, when 5...c5 can now be met by 6 c3. Note that, just as in the Advance Variation, maintaining the pawn chain is more important than speedy development; White can get away with extravagances such as Nce2 as the position in the centre is so blocked (White wishes to develop with f2-f4, Nf3, g2-g3, Bg2 etc). Another, more free-flowing, way to play the position for White is with 5 f4! c5 6 Nf3. In this situation White is happy enough to recapture on d4 with a piece because the pawn on e5 has vital protection from f4.

4 e5

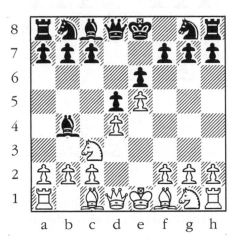

After 4 Bd3 Black can release the tension with 4...dxe4 5 Bxe4 and then gain time by attacking the e4-bishop with 5...Nf6!.

The other obvious way to keep the tension is with 4 Bd2 but then White must be prepared to sacrifice a pawn or two because following 4...dxe4 the d4-pawn is en prise so 5 Nxe4 can be met by 5...Qxd4! (4...Bxc3 5 Bxc3 dxe4 doesn't win a pawn, as White has the double attack 6 Qg4!). Instead White follows up with 5 Qg4 (this attack on the unprotected g7-pawn crops up time and time again in the Winawer) when Black must choose between grabbing another pawn and entering the complications after 5...Qxd4 6 0-0-0, or offering his g-pawn in return for rapid development and gaining time on White's queen after 5...Nf6 6 Qxg7 Rg8 7 Qh6.

4...c5!

Again we see this pawn break. Now White usually acts fast to ensure that his centre doesn't crumble by playing...

5 a3 Bxc3+ 6 bxc3

Once more comparisons can be made with the Advance Variation. There are, however, two significant differences:

1) Because of the doubled c-pawns, White's pawn structure is weaker.

2) Black no longer has his dark-squared bishop, probably his strongest minor piece, certainly stronger than the bishop on c8.

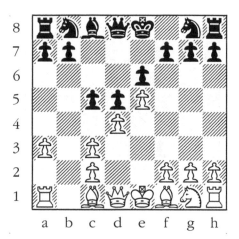

There are many variations in this complex line, one of the most interesting being...

6...Qc7 7 Qg4 Ne7!?

If Black doesn't want to give up the g7-pawn then 7...f5 is a good move.

8 Qxg7 Rg8 9 Qxh7 cxd4!

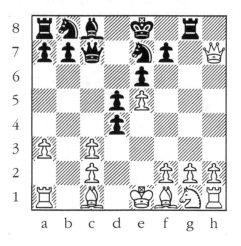

10 Ne2

Not 10 cxd4?? Qc3+! forking king and rook.

10...Nbc6 11 f4!

11 cxd4 Nxd4! was the point to Black's previous move: 12 Nxd4 allows 12...Qc3+!.

11...dxc3 12 Qd3 Bd7

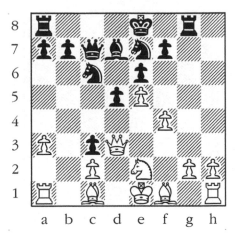

White will capture on c3 leaving him a pawn ahead, but speedy development and active pieces make this a fun line for Black to play, even if objectively White is probably better.

The Caro-Kann and the Scandinavian

1 e4 c6 2 d4 d5

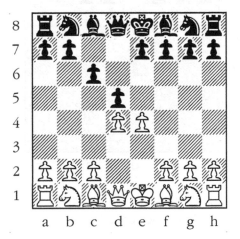

The Caro-Kann is very similar to the French in that, initially at least, Black bases his central strategy on a strongpoint around d5. One of the main differences to the French is that by not playing ...e7-e6, Black keeps the c8-h3 diagonal free and can hope to develop his light-squared bishop actively.

Another opening worth mentioning here, because it is very similar to the Caro-Kann (it has the same pawn structure) is the Scandinavian, which begins 1...d5 2 exd5 Qxd5. Black's idea with 1...d5 is to immediately open lines for his pieces and thus ensure easy development. The price he pays is that he loses time having to move his queen again after 3 Nc3. Play typically continues 3...Qa5 4 d4 Nf6 5 Nf3 Bf5 6 Bd2 c6! (ensuring a safe retreat for the queen) 7 Bc4 e6.

3 Nc3

If White plays an Advanced Variation with 3 e5 then Black continues with 3...Bf5.

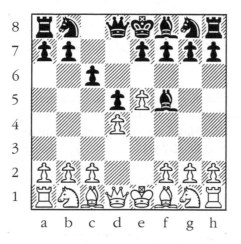

The plan is to continue with ...e7-e6, ...c7-c5, ...Nc6 etc. as in the French Advance but with a far more active bishop on f5. At first sight this seems like a big improvement for Black, but the sword is doubled-edged. For one thing Black's play against White's centre is considerably slower (one tempo is spent on ...Bf5, another on taking two moves with the c-pawn to reach c5). Another thing is that, whilst being more active on f5, the bishop is also more prone to attack, and White has at his disposal a number of aggressive lines based on harassing the bishop, 4 Nc3 e6 5 g4 Bg6 6 Nge2 c5 7 h4 being the most popular.

3...dxe4!?

By far Black's most popular move, even though it seems inconsistent with the previous two. Logically you would think Black would want to keep the strongpoint on d5, but in fact there are few ways to do this without some compromise required.

3...e6?!, whilst being super-solid, clearly contradicts Black's philosophy of finding an active role for the c8-bishop. If Black were going to play this move he should have done so on move one (the French), not wasting a tempo with ...c6.

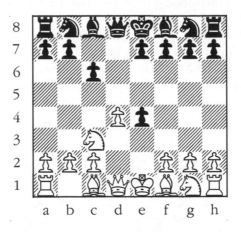

With ...Bb4 being unavailable, the only way to both keep the tension and attack e4 is with 3...Nf6?!. The problem is that after 4 e5! Black's knight doesn't have a useful square to go to. After 4...Ne4 5 Nxe4 dxe4 Black will always be worried that his e4-pawn might be rounded up (6 Ne2 followed by Nc3 or Ng3 makes sense). That leaves 4...Nfd7 but then it proves far too cumbersome for Black to move this knight again, play ...Bf5, ...e6 and finally ...c5. Added to this, Black also has to be wary of the disruptive pawn sacrifice 5 e6!? fxe6 6 Bd3.

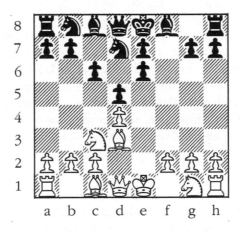

This looks pretty uncomfortable for Black, and 6...e5?? loses immediately to 7 Qh5+ g6 8 Qxg6+! hxg6 9 Bxg6 – a very nice mate to play if allowed!

So, in the final analysis, 3...Nf6 doesn't really cut it. If Black wishes to keep the tension and an unblocked c8-h3 diagonal, then the best bet is 3...g6!?, for example 4 Nf3 Bg7 5 h3 (to prevent ...Bg4) and now Black can return to typical Caro play with 5...dxe4 6 Nxe4 Nd7 intending ...Ngf6, or else try his luck in the complications after 5...Nf6!? 6 e5 (6 Bd3 is quieter) 6...Ne4 7 Nxe4 dxe4 8 Ng5 c5!.

4 Nxe4

This position was discussed quite thoroughly in Chapter 4 (see Exercise 3). The extra possibility I wish to cover here is...

4...Nd7

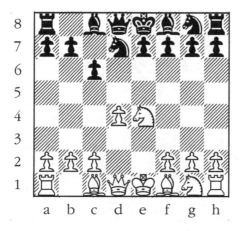

Together with 4...Bf5, this is Black's most popular continuation in tournament play. Initially it makes a strange impression to block the c8-bishop, but Black hopes that the knight won't remain on this square for too long. The main point of 4...Nd7 is to prepare ...Ngf6. Black's idea is that a trade on f6 can now be met by ...Ndxf6, avoiding doubled pawns and freeing the c8-bishop. This strategy works well if we simply continue with logical-looking moves from both sides. For example, 5 Nf3 Ngf6 6 Nxf6+ Nxf6 7 Bc4 Bf5! (but not 7...Bg4?? allowing the trick 8 Bxf7+! Kxf7 9 Ne5+) 8 0-0 e6.

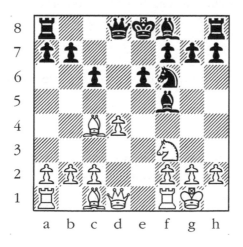

Black will develop his f8-bishop and castle, when his development problems are completely solved.

Because of the ease of Black's development in lines such as this, theory considers White's most promising approach to be one that combines development with constraining:

5 Bc4 Ngf6 6 Ng5!

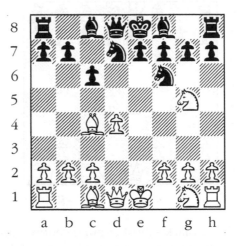

Mate in one is threatened. Okay, this is easy to prevent with...

6...e6

...but there's a cost: Black's bishop on c8 is now blocked in. The trade-off is that the knight has already moved three times and will soon be forced to move again after ...h6. Let's just go on a few moves further:

7 Qe2!

This move contains a devilish threat. If Black is too hasty in chasing away the g5-knight he pays heavily: 7...h6? 8 Nxf7! Kxf7 9 Qxe6+ Kg6 10 Bd3+ Kh5 11 Qh3 mate!

7...Nb6!

Now of course 9 Nxf7 doesn't work because e6 is protected by the bishop on c8.

8 Bb3

8 Bd3 is just as playable.

8...h6!

Grabbing the d4-pawn is too greedy on this occasion. Following 8...Qxd4? 9 N1f3 queen retreats are met by 10 Ne5! doubling up on the f7-pawn, while 9...Bb4+ 10 c3 Bxc3+ is met not by 11 bxc3? Qxc3+ but by 11 Kf1! and then 12 bxc3.

9 N5f3

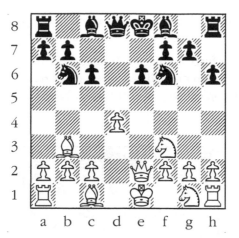

...and now a logical way for Black to continue is to break in the centre with 9...c5.

For a long time 5 Bc4 was considered the main line against 5...Nd7, but then around twenty years ago it was discovered that White had another possibility in the form of the paradoxical...

5 Ng5!?

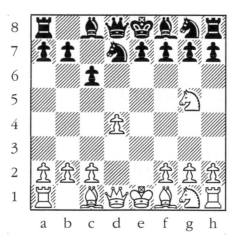

This seems to contradict all the guidelines, but just like 5 Bc4 Ngf6 6 Ng5, White is trying to restrict Black's development. The justification behind this move is that it's not so easy to kick the knight away, the obvious 5...h6?! being met by the surprising 6 Ne6! – 6...fxe6?? allows checkmate with 7 Qh5+ g6 8 Qxg6. Instead Black normally continues with...

5...Ngf6

Now White can transpose to 5 Bc4 with 6 Bc4, but more popular is...

6 Bd3

Here 6...h6?! still doesn't force a knight retreat: after 7 Ne6 the knight is immune on account of 7...fxe6?? 8 Bg6 mate. Black often plays 6...e6, but if he wishes to develop his c8-bishop the logical way to continue looks to be the continuation 6...Nb6 7 N1f3 Bg4.

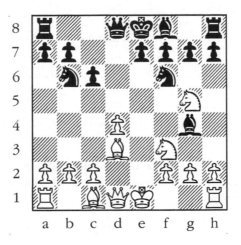

Black must be ready to answer 8 Nxf7!? not with 8...Kxf7?, which runs into 9 Ne5+!, but 8...Bxf3!. The tactical sequence 9 Nxd8 Bxd1 10 Ne6 Bg4 11 Nc7+ Kd7 12 Nxa8 Nxa8 leads to roughly equal position.

Queen's Gambit Declined

1 d4 d5 2 c4

We came across the Queen's Gambit in Chapters 4 and 5. Here I'll simply expand on some of the early moves in the main line.

2...e6

If Black is going to decline the gambit, then this is the most solid way to do so. Basically, Black refuses to give any ground away in the centre: if White captures on d5 then Black is ready to recapture with the pawn, thus keeping control of the important central squares. The only real problem with 2...e6 is that it blocks in the c8-bishop. In many Queen's Gambit Declined (QGD) variations one of Black's major issues is how to activate this piece.

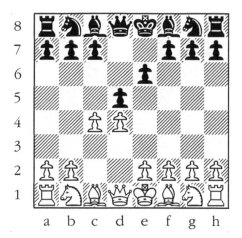

2...Nf6?! would be a mistake due to 3 cxd5! Nxd5 (or 3...Qxd5 4 Nc3) 4 Nf3 and White is going to follow up with e2-e4, erecting an ideal centre and gaining time on Black's knight in the process. After, say 4...e6 5 e4 Nf6 6 Nc3

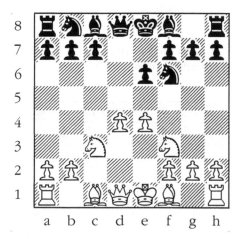

we have actually transposed to Kasparov-Rebelo (see page 142). Note that the immediate 4 e4 is tempting but a slight inaccuracy: after 4...Nf6 5 Nc3 e5! Black gets more counterplay than he deserves (6 dxe5 Qxd1+ 7 Kxd1 Ng4!).

If Black's philosophy favours active piece play over maintaining the centre, then a better way to do this is with 2...Nc6!?, which is known as the Chigorin Defence. The point is that following 3 cxd5 (certainly not forced; 3 Nf3 and 3 Nc3 are alternatives) 3...Qxd5 White must do something about the threat to the d4-pawn, and this gives Black enough time to organize rapid development, e.g. 4 Nf3 e5! 5 Nc3 Bb4! 6 Bd2 Bxc3 7 Bxc3 e4; or 4 e3 e5! 5 Nc3 Bb4! 6 Bd2 Bxc3 7 bxc3 Nf6.

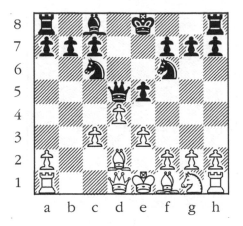

In this second variation the position becomes a battle between White's impressive pawn centre and Black's active piece development.

3 Nc3 Nf6 4 Bg5

Here's that pin again. Unlike 1 e4 openings, in the Queen's Gambit White generally develops his queenside pieces first.

4...Be7

Black can also choose to support the f6-knight with 4...Nbd7!? which contains a sneaky trick: 5 cxd5 exd5 6 Nxd5?? (why not?)

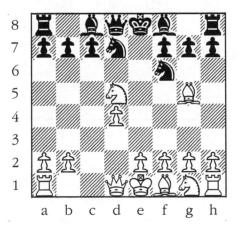

6...Nxd5!! 7 Bxd8 Bb4+! (that's why!) and now White's only move is 8 Qd2 but following 8...Bxd2+ 9 Kxd2 Kxd8 Black is a piece for a pawn ahead.

5 e3

Now that the c1-bishop has moved to g5, White makes room for his other bishop.

5...0-0 6 Nf3 h6 7 Bh4

7 Bxf6 Bxf6 is also possible but White usually prefers to keep this bishop, for the time being at least.

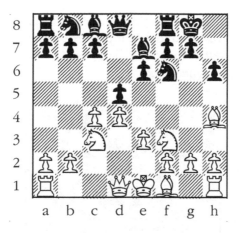

The position after 7 Bh4 is a major starting point for play in the Queen's Gambit Declined. Black's main concern is how to effectively develop his queenside pieces, and in particular the perennial problem piece on c8. One major option for Black here is to ease his slightly cramped position via a couple of exchanges with...

7...Ne4! 8 Bxe7 Qxe7

Now following 9 cxd5 Black avoids losing a pawn by playing the zwischenzug 9...Nxc3 and after 10 bxc3 exd5 things are much brighter because the c8-bishop finally has a clear path to develop. Another natural way for White to continue is with 9 Bd3, adding pressure to e4 and preparing to castle. Following 9...Nxc3 10 bxc3 Black solves the problem of the c8-bishop in another way: 10...dxc4! 11 Bxc4 b6!...

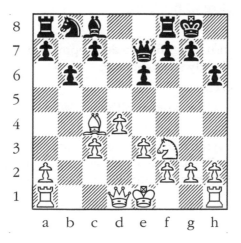

...followed by ...Bb7 when the bishop reaches a nice, long diagonal.

The line 9 Nxe4 dxe4 10 Nd2 is also not to be feared in view of 10...e5! when again Black can develop freely. More testing, though, is...

9 Rc1!

...activating the rook on the c-file. One of the points is that after 9...Nxc3 10 Rxc3 dxc4 11 Bxc4 White has managed to develop more economically (the bishop has reached c4 in one move rather than two). So instead the main line goes...

9...Nxc3 10 Rxc3 c6 11 Bd3 Nd7 12 0-0

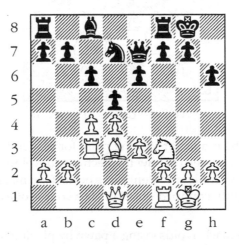

Here Black has two ways to try to solve the problem of the c8-bishop. One is to play 12...dxc4 13 Bxc4 b6 with the idea of ...Bb7 and eventually ...c5. The more classical approach is...

12...e5

...threatening to win a piece with ...e5-e4.

13 dxe5 dxc4

13...Nxe5 14 cxd5 cxd5 also solves Black's development problems but Black would prefer not to have that slightly weak d-pawn.

14 Bxc4 Nxe5 15 Nxe5 Qxe5

...and finally the bishop is free to move, although White's slightly greater activity still promises an edge.

Going back to Black's seventh move, a more sophisticated option that's popular amongst grandmasters is 7...b6, immediately addressing the problem of the c8-bishop. Play could easily continue 8 Bd3 Bb7 9 0-0 Nbd7 when Black is fully mobilized.

The Slav

1 d4 d5 2 c4 c6

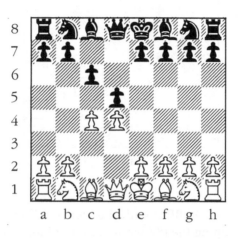

Just like the Queen's Gambit Declined could be related to the French Defence, the Slav is the sister opening to the Caro-Kann. Ideally Black would like to play in QGD fashion, but with the light-squared bishop developed actively outside the pawn chain rather than stuck behind it. Some young players looking for a defence to the Queen's Gambit are initially attracted by this possibility, even though if White plays accurately Black cannot favourably achieve this idealistic formation (chess isn't easy!). Even so, the Slav is still a very playable opening.

3 Nf3 Nf6

As well as leaving the c8-h3 diagonal free for the moment, another feature of ...c7-c6 is that Black is in a more favourable position to grab the c4-pawn with ...dxc4, and White certainly has to be wary of this possibility. The point is that ...c7-c6 supports the advance ...b7-b5 which in turn is what Black needs to play if he wants to try to hold on to the extra pawn. For the moment White doesn't have to be afraid: 3...dxc4 4 e3 b5 5 a4!

(see following diagram)

(White must try to break up the pawn chain before Black consolidates) 5...a6 6 axb5 cxb5 7 b3 and White wins the pawn back by force after 7...cxb3 8 Bxb5+!. Even so, Black can still play in this fashion, substituting 5...a6 with 5...e6 6 axb5 cxb5 7 b3 Bb4+! 8 Bd2 Bxd2+ 9 Nbxd2 a5! 10 bxc4 b4. I do like White's lead in development and pawn centre here, but Black's two passed pawns on the queenside cannot be totally ignored.

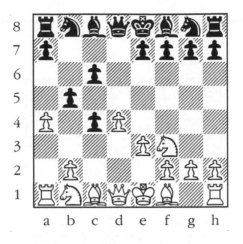

4 Nc3 dxc4!

The idealistic move here is 4...Bf5?! with the idea of following up in QGD fashion with ...e7-e6, developing the f8-bishop, castling kingside etc. with a very reasonable position; in fact, no worries at all. This is all very well if White allows this, but he can throw a hefty spanner into the works with 5 cxd5! cxd5 6 Qb3!, when trying to keep b7 and d5 defended at the same time gives Black a real headache.

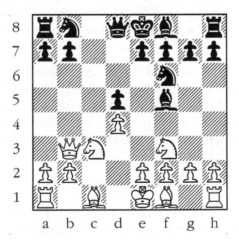

6...Qb6 loses a pawn to 7 Nxd5! Qxb3 8 Nxf6+! exf6 9 axb3, while 6...b6 weakens the queenside, after which the pawn sacrifice 7 e4! is very strong. For instance, 7...dxe4 8 Ne5! e6 9 Bb5+! Nbd7 10 Bg5 and the pins are decisive: 10...Be7 11 Bxf6 Bxf6 12 Nxd7 etc.

With 4...Bf5 ruled out, Black utilizes the other idea behind 2...c6: grabbing the pawn on c4. White has to make a decision here: either occupy the centre but forgo regaining the pawn, or take steps to ensure winning the pawn back but allow Black to develop the c8-bishop to f5. The second option is the favourite choice in tournament play.

5 a4

Preventing ...b5. Instead 5 e4!? is certainly possible, but following 5...b5! it's a real gambit, the main line running 6 e5 (6 a4 b4 and the e4-pawn will hang) 6...Nd5 7 a4 e6, and after 8 axb5 Black keeps his extra pawn following the zwischenzug 8...Nxc3 9 bxc3 cxb5.

5...Bf5 6 Ne5

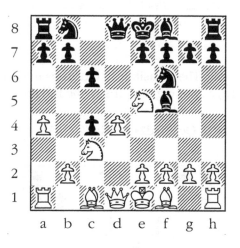

The most ambitious move, with White still looking for central domination with f2-f3 followed by e2-e4. Another common line runs 6 e3 e6 7 Bxc4 Bb4! 8 0-0 Nbd7.

6...e6

I'm giving this as the main line, although more recently 6...Nbd7 7 Nxc4 Qc7 planning ...e7-e5, has been fashionable. Theory runs 8 g3! (preparing both Bg2 and Bf4) 8...e5 9 dxe5 Nxe5 10 Bf4 Nfd7 11 Bg2 and now either of the moves 11...f6 or 11...g5!?.

7 f3 Bb4 8 e4 Bxe4!

Not really a sacrifice as such, as Black obtains a few pawns for the bishop. 8...Bg6 is possible of course, but following 9 Bxc4 Black has no real compensation for White's super-strong centre.

9 fxe4 Nxe4

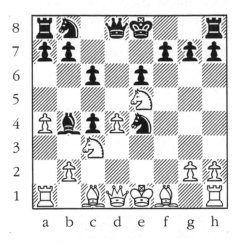

10 Bd2

White must tread carefully. The plausible 10 Qc2 runs into the nice tactic
10...Nxc3! 11 bxc3 Qxd4!, exploiting the pins to the full and winning lots of material.

10...Qxd4 11 Nxe4 Qxe4+ 12 Qe2 Bxd2+ 13 Kxd2 Qd5+

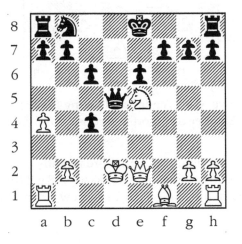

Now White usually plays 14 Kc2 and takes the c4-pawn next move. Black will still
have three pawns for the bishop and White's king remains out in the open. That
said, Black doesn't have that many pieces to attack with so it's not overly vulnerable. It takes strong nerves to play this position as White but if the queens are
traded White can look forward to good chances in the endgame.

The Dutch

1 d4 f5

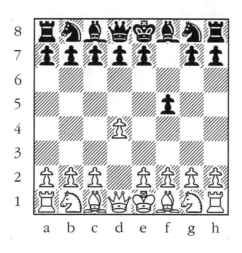

It would be remiss of me not to mention the Dutch Defence, a kind of mirror image of the Sicilian in which Black prevents e2-e4 and sets up an asymmetrical pawn structure. You've probably already guessed why the Dutch Defence is far less popular than the Sicilian. Yes, not everyone is happy weakening the king by moving the f-pawn on the very first move! However, there's also an advantage that's worth mentioning. Compared with the Sicilian where White typically plays an early d2-d4, White finds it difficult to force e2-e4 under favourable circumstances.

2 c4

As in the Queen's Gambit, White's most popular option is to gain space in the centre with this move.

2 Nc3, intending e2-e4, is playable, but this advance cannot be forced through, e.g. 2...d5 (2...Nf6 3 Bg5 d5 is also played) and now if White wants to play e4 he should play it as a gambit with 3 e4!? dxe4 (3...fxe4? 4 Qh5+! g6 5 Qxd5) 4 f3, rather than trying to arrange it with 3 f3. Apparently the complications arising after 3...c5! 4 e4 e5!...

(see following diagram)

...are not unfavourable for Black (you'll have to believe me on this one!).

2...Nf6 3 g3

The kingside fianchetto is very popular against the Dutch. If White plays more classically, say with 3 Nc3 e6 4 Nf3 then a good idea for Black is to play in Nimzo-

Indian style with 4...Bb4! when he keeps a grip on the e4-square (compare this with the Nimzo-Indian line we looked at in Chapter 5).

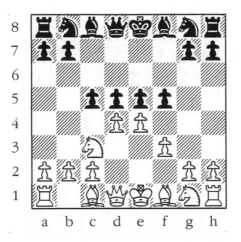

3...e6

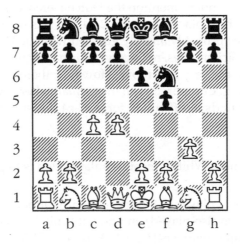

Black can play in a more sophisticated way with 3...g6 aiming to reach a set-up similar to the King's Indian but with the added ...f7-f5. Here, though, I wish to cover the line which in my experience is the most popular amongst improving players: the Stonewall.

4 Bg2 d5

Now there is no chance of White playing e2-e4, at least in the foreseeable future.

5 Nf3 c6 6 0-0 Bd6

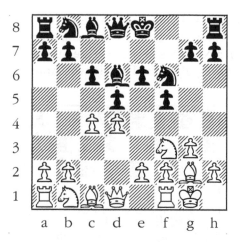

A typical position for the Stonewall Dutch. Black has a vice-like grip on e4 and this is the major positive. On the other hand, there's also a couple of negatives: the hole on e5 and the problem of what to do with the bishop on c8. With a blocked pawn structure, play tends to be slow and positional rather than tactical.

The King's Indian

1 d4 Nf6 2 c4 g6

This fianchetto signals the hypermodern King's Indian Defence, in which Black concentrates on speedy development and leaves the battle for the centre until later.

3 Nc3

There's no reason for White not to aim for a large centre with e2-e4.

3...Bg7 4 e4

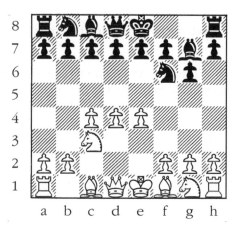

4...d6 5 Nf3

5 e5?! holds no fears for Black. Following 5...dxe5! 6 dxe5 Qxd1+ 7 Nxd1 Ng4 Black is ahead in development and the pawn on e5 is vulnerable. White does, however, have options other than 5 Nf3. One of these is the hugely ambitious 5 f4, which you could probably guess is called the Four Pawns Attack.

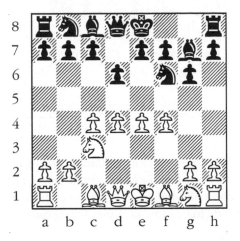

This line, in which White goes for total central domination, is certainly playable, but there are risks involved, for example 5...0-0 6 Nf3 c5! (striking back) 7 e5? 7...Nfd7! and no matter what White does his centre collapses and all that remains are weaknesses – I particularly like the line 8 e6 fxe6 9 Ng5 cxd4! 10 Nxe6 Qa5!. Or there's 7 dxc5 Qa5! 8 cxd6? (8 Bd3!) 8...Nxe4! 9 dxe7 Re8 10 Bd2 Nxc3 11 Bxc3 Bxc3+ 12 bxc3 Rxe7+ 13 Be2 Qxc3+ and again White's position is a total mess. It's certainly not all doom and gloom after 5 f4 – there are good ways to play this position for White. With these variations I just wanted to emphasize some of the resources of Black's opening.

5...0-0 6 Be2 e5!

Now Black is fully developed on the kingside, it's time to strike back in the centre.

7 0-0

At first sight it seems that White can win a pawn here. However, following 7 dxe5 dxe5 8 Qxd8 Rxd8 9 Nxe5 Black can unleash a discovered attack to win back the pawn. After 9...Nxe4! 10 Nxe4 Bxe5 Black has maintained material equality and has a perfectly good position. Note that the desperado 10 Nxf7?, hoping for 10...Kxf7 11 Nxe4, fails to 10...Bxc3+! 11 bxc3 Kxf7 when Black is a piece ahead.

7...Nc6

Adding further pressure to White's pawn on d4. White usually releases this pressure by advancing.

8 d5 Ne7

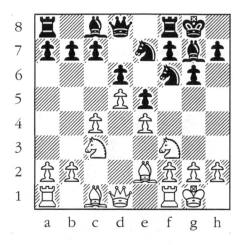

The King's Indian is similar to the French Defence in that the centre often becomes blocked. Just as in the French, White has a little more space, but Black has a solid position. The King's Indian appeals to aggressive players because generally Black's main plan in this position is a kingside attack, whereas White usually plays on the other side of the board. Of Black's two pawn breaks, ...c7-c6 and ...f7-f5, it's the latter that is usually carried out. Meanwhile, White will aim for his own pawn break with c4-c5 to help him open lines on the queenside. There are numerous complicated lines from this position; one that illustrates the typical play is...

9 Ne1 Ne8 10 Be3 f5 11 f3 f4 12 Bf2 g5 13 c5 h5

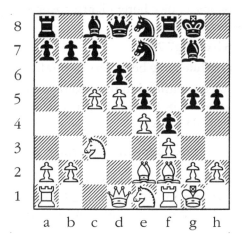

...when both attacks are well under way. The King's Indian is a difficult opening to master, but the rewards can be very high. For those willing to try, I can recommend Joe Gallagher's classic *Starting Out: The King's Indian*.

The Grünfeld

1 d4 Nf6 2 c4 g6 3 Nc3 d5

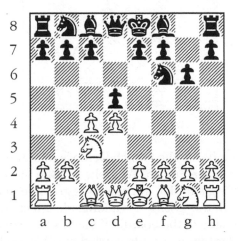

This is the move that introduces the Grünfeld Defence, another opening from the hypermodern school of chess. Black offers to trade his d-pawn for White's c-pawn and in doing so he gives White the opportunity of establishing an impressive-looking centre. Black, however, hopes that in fact this centre will be vulnerable to attack.

Again White has considerable choice here; I'll just cover a few possibilities in the line that looks the most logical:

4 cxd5 Nxd5 5 e4 Nxc3 6 bxc3 Bg7 7 Nf3

So far all the moves from White have been very natural.

White can avoid the problems outlined in the next note by developing his knight to the more passive e2-square: 7 Bc4 c5 8 Ne2! (the reason for this move becomes clear later) 8...0-0 9 0-0 Nc6 10 Be3 Bg4.

(see following diagram)

With the knight on f3, this pin would have been very awkward, but now White can play 11 f3! when theory continues 11...Na5! 12 Bd3 cxd4 13 cxd4 Be6 with a complicated struggle. It's true White still has central control, but Black's pieces are quite actively placed.

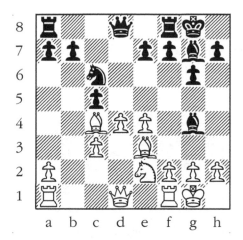

7...c5!

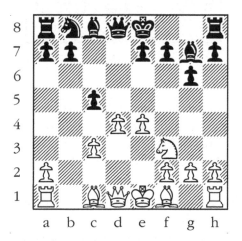

This pawn move is a crucial part of Black's strategy, which is to gang up on the d-pawn as quickly as possible and try to induce a weakness in White's centre. Of course both 8 dxc5? and 8 d5? allow 8...Bxc3+ – this illustrates the power of Black's bishop down the long diagonal.

8 Rb1!

This would be quite a difficult move to find just by playing the opening on general principles. At first sight it looks a bit unusual to develop this rook so early, but White is moving it off the long a1-h8 diagonal in order to avoid certain tactics that Black has at his disposal.

Normal development with 8 Be2 is okay but it allows Black to carry out his plan:

8...Nc6! 9 Be3 (9 d5!? Bxc3+ 10 Bd2 Bxa1 11 Qxa1 Nd4 12 Nxd4 cxd4 13 Qxd4 f6 leaves Black rook for bishop ahead, although it's true that White's imposing centre gives him some compensation for this material loss) 9...Bg4 and now due to the pressure on d4, White is forced to compromise his pawn front with 10 e5 and the resulting position is roughly equal.

8...0-0 9 Be2

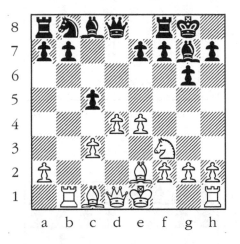

9...Nc6

Another main line runs 9...cxd4 10 cxd4 Qa5+ 11 Bd2 Qxa2 (a cheeky pawn-grab) 12 0-0, when White's better development and strong pawn centre gives him clear compensation for the pawn, but Black has no obvious weaknesses. In the final analysis, this may well be Black's best bet in this line.

10 d5

Finally White feels obliged to move one of the central duo, but at least this comes with a gain of time on Black's knight.

Following 10 Be3 Black can consider playing as in the previous note with 10...cxd4 11 cxd4 Qa5+ 12 Bd2 Qxa2.

10...Ne5

Black can also grab a pawn with 10...Bxc3+ but following 11 Bd2 Bxd2+ 12 Qxd2 Na5 White can begin a dangerous attack on the black king with 13 h4!, intending h4-h5 and Qh6 etc.

11 Nxe5 Bxe5

Black has forced the d-pawn to advance but White's centre is still quite strong, enough to give him an edge in a sharp position.

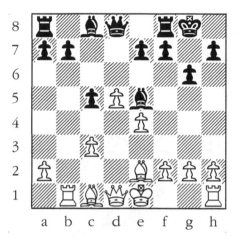

The English Opening

1 c4

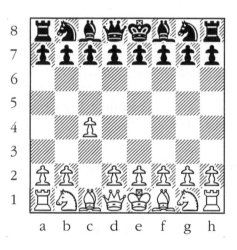

The English Opening is another that belongs to the hypermodern school. It also often simply transposes into 1 d4 openings, for example 1...Nf6 2 Nc3 g6 3 e4 Bg7 4 d4 and we have reached a King's Indian (although notice that White has sneakily avoided allowing the possibility of the Grünfeld by using this move order).

Black's most popular independent choice after 1 c4 is...

1...e5

...reaching for all intents and purposes a reversed Sicilian. One popular line continues...

2 Nc3 Nf6 3 Nf3 Nc6 4 g3

Here Black must make a decision whether to develop with 4...Bb4 or 4...Bc5, or play in Open Sicilian fashion with...

4...d5 5 cxd5 Nxd5 6 Bg2

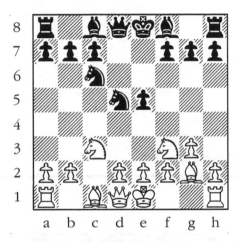

Now we have a reversed Dragon. It's important to note that the extra move, coupled with the fact that White has not committed himself to d2-d3, alters things considerably from the mainline Dragon. For starters, White already threatens some damage with a discovered attack (6...Be7? 7 Nxe5! Nxc3 – 7...Nxe5 8 Nxd5 – 8 Bxc6+ bxc6 9 dxc3 wins a pawn). Secondly, if Black tries to play as he does in the mainline Dragon, he gets a bit of a shock:

6...Be6 7 0-0 f6

Now instead of 8 d3, followed by Bd2, Rc1 etc, White can lash out in the centre with...

8 d4!

(see following diagram)

...when Black's lag in development and the weakness of ...f6 become serious issues after, say, 8...exd4 9 Nxd4 Nxd4 10 Qxd4.

Going back to move six, it makes more sense for Black to play quietly with 6...Nb6!, preventing both any Nxe5 tactics and an early d2-d4, followed by ...Be7 and ...0-0.

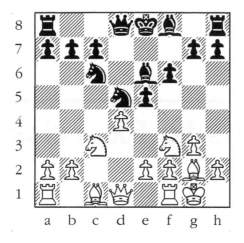

Solutions to Exercises

Chapter One

1) 16

2) a) 6; b) 8; c) 4.

3) 1 e4, 1 c4 and 1 Nc3 all control the d5-square.

4) After 1 d4 Black could prevent White from playing 2 e4 with 1...d5, 1...f5 or 1...Nf6.

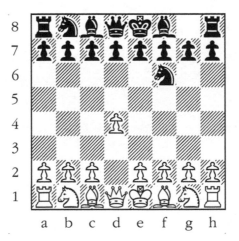

Chapter Two

1) Of course White could prevent ...Qxg2 with, say, 3 Qf3 or 3 g3, but White can

really punish Black for his early queen move with...

3 Nf3! Qxg2

Otherwise what was the point of 2...Qg5 apart from to lose time?

4 Rg1 Qh3

Now White has the tactic...

5 Bxf7+!

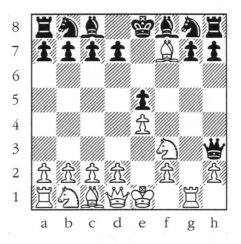

The point is that 5...Kxf7 allows a deadly knight fork with 6 Ng5+. Black can struggle on with 5...Kd8 but following 6 d4! he is way behind in development, has lost his castling rights and is in danger of being totally overwhelmed. Note that 6...exd4 loses to 7 Rg3!, trapping the queen – a suitable punishment for its very hopeful sortie.

2) (a) 5-4 in White's favour (remember that castling counts as a developing move and pieces that have been traded should be ignored); (b) 4-4. Black's queen because it is back on its starting square, even though it has moved twice. Also, the knight on e5 only counts as one developing move.

Chapter Three

1) 1 e4, 2 Nf3, 3 Bc4 and 4 0-0...

(see following diagram)

...or anything similar would do the trick. Alternatively White could fianchetto: 1 g3, 2 Bg2, 3 Nf3 and 4 0-0.

2) At first sight there doesn't seem to anything disastrously wrong with 5 Nge2?, especially as White seems to be on the verge of making his king safe via castling, but...

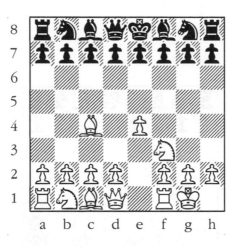

5...Ng4!

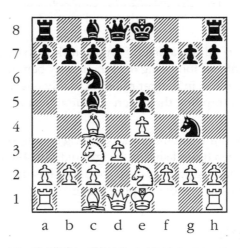

The same type of attack on the f-pawn that has been discussed earlier. But can't White just castle out of trouble?

6 0-0?

Before going on to see the problem with this natural move, it's worth pointing out the alternatives. 6 Rf1 loses a pawn to 6...Nxh2, while 6 Be3 Bxe3 7 fxe3 Nxe3 is even worse. White must lose a pawn, but the best way to do so is with 6 d4 when Black should reply with 6...exd4! (6...Nxd4? 7 Nxd4! uncovers an attack on g4).

6...Qh4!

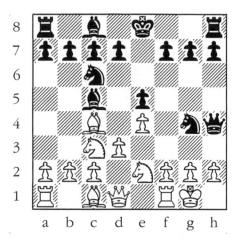

The sting in the tail! The f2-pawn is attacked for a third time and, crucially, Black has an even more devastating threat: ...Qxh2 mate. So White must give up the f2-pawn, and more must follow.

7 h3 Nxf2!

Both attacking the queen on d1 and lining up a crushing discovered or double check. White really has to give up more material with 8 Rxf2 Qxf2+ because 8 Qe1, for example, allows mate after 8...Nxh3+ 9 Kh2 Nf2+ 10 Kg1 Qh1.

The crucial difference between 5 Nge2? and 5 Nf3! is that following the latter, 5...Ng4 can be confidently met by 6 0-0 because Black no longer has 6...Qh4 available.

Chapter Four

1) No! Black has the straightforward answer to the threat with...

7...Rc8

...protecting the c7-square, and White has no follow-up to justify the aggression on his previous move. Following, say...

8 0-0

...Black can simply force the knight to retreat with...

8...a6

...and after 9 Nc3 White has lost time: in effect Black has played the 'free' moves ...Rc8 and ...a7-a6, both of which are fairly useful.

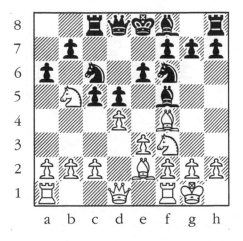

2) No it's not! After the obvious...

7 Re1!

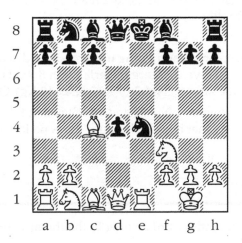

...pinning the knight to the king, Black is in real trouble. If 7...Bf5 White can play 8 Ng5! with the double threat of Nxf7 and Nxe4. Black could instead try...

7...f5

...but this is clearly undesirable, as with g8 covered Black no longer has the option of kingside castling. Now 8 Ng5! is still very strong, as is...

8 Nbd2!

...when Black has little hope of surviving many moves, For example:

8...Bb4

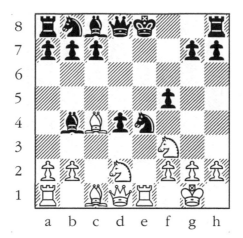

Or 8...Qe7 9 Nxe4 fxe4 10 Bg5! and the queen cannot remain protecting the e4-pawn.

9 Nxe4!

Black can take the rook on e1, but White's remaining pieces will swarm around Black's airy king.

9...Bxe1 10 Bg5! Qd7 11 Qxe1 fxe4 12 Qxe4+ Kf8 13 Qf4+ Ke8 14 Re1+

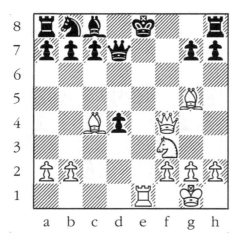

...when Black must give up his queen and will soon be mated.

3) A move crying out to be played here is **4...Bf5!**, both developing a piece and creating a threat, and it's no surprise that this move is popular in tournament chess. Let's look at possible replies for White:

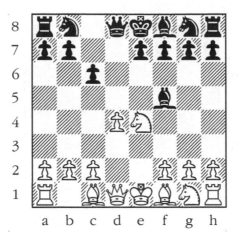

a) 5 Ng3! is the reply that is seen most often: White's knight turns the tables and it's now the bishop that is under attack.

Question: Is White threatening to win a piece?

Answer: Actually, no! It's easy to miss, but at the moment Nxf5 can be met by ...Qa5+ followed by ...Qxf5.

However, Black reasons that the bishop on f5 is a slightly stronger piece than the g3-knight and so is reluctant to allow this trade. In view of this, Black normally retreats with 5...Bg6.

b) 5 Nc5 is another option that should be considered, White's idea being to gain time by attacking the b7-pawn.

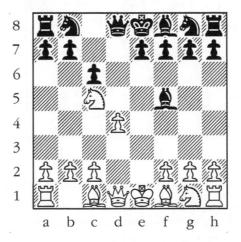

Of course after 5...b6 the knight would have to move again. Added to this, it's always worth checking how 'real' a threat is. Following 5...Nd7!? White can capture on b7, but after 6 Nxb7 Qb6 White is forced to play 7 Nc5 when Black can regain the pawn with 7...Nxc5 8 dxc5 Qxc5.

c) 5 Bd3!? both develops a piece and defends the knight, but White has to be prepared to sacrifice the d-pawn after 5...Qxd4. It's true that following this White can gain time on Black's queen with 6 Nf3 but after 6...Qd8, sensibly moving the queen out of any trouble, it's not clear how much compensation White has for the pawn.

d) 5 Qf3 also defends the knight on e4, and it attacks the bishop.

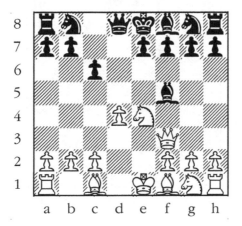

Black could trade on e4, but probably the strongest move here is 5...e6!, defending the bishop and preparing further development.

Going back to Black's options on move four after 1 e4 c6 2 d4 d5 3 Nc3 dxe4 4 Nxe4, the other straightforward way to develop 'with tempo' is with **4...Nf6**.

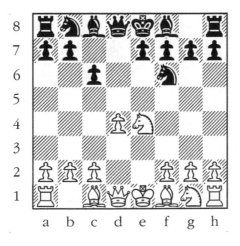

The obvious reply to this is...

5 Nxf6+!

...because, compared to say, 5 Nc3 or 5 Ng3, White isn't losing any time (Black has to recapture before carrying on with development!). Interestingly, many of the junior students I showed this position to were wary of 4...Nf6 because Black is forced to accept doubled pawns (more about these in Chapter 5). However, I would consider the position after...

5...exf6

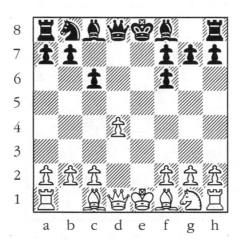

...to be one that is good for an improving player to accept as Black. The open lines mean that development is straightforward (inexperienced players tend to go wrong more easily when the development procedure is complicated) and the doubled f-pawns could provide vital extra cover for the black king once it has castled kingside.

Question: After the logical move 6 Bc4, Black can play the tricky 6...Qe7+!?.

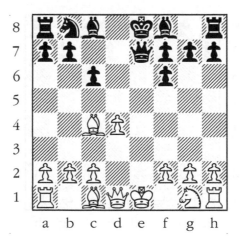

Should White respond with 7 Ne2, 7 Be3 or 7 Qe2 here?

Answer: Definitely 7 Qe2; both 7 Ne2?? and 7 Be3?? are blunders, after which Black wins the c4-bishop with 7...Qb4+!. I repeat: never miss a check!

If Black were looking for more adventure, then 5...gxf6!? would be a double-edged way to play.

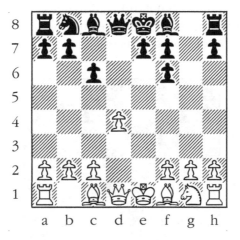

The most important thing to realize from Black's point of view here is that his kingside is substantially weakened by this recapture, so the best course of action for the black king is to castle queenside. Black can then utilize the open g-file in a positive way by placing his rook on g8. A typical sequence here would be 6 Nf3 Bg4 7 Be2 Qc7 8 0-0 Nd7 when Black will follow up with ...0-0-0.

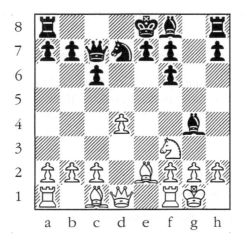

As well as the obvious 5 Nxf6+, White has one or two alternatives:

a) 5 Bd3?! develops a piece and protects the knight, but again it leaves the important d4-pawn hanging to Black's queen.

b) 5 Qd3!? is another move that defends the knight, and here White is on the way to castling queenside. One sensible approach for Black is 5...Nxe4 6 Qxe4 Nd7! when the queen's knight replaces its vanquished partner on the desirable f6-square and will gain time on the white queen when doing so.

In fact 5 Qd3 isn't a great move, but it did lead to one of the most celebrated finishes of all time: 5...e5? 6 dxe5 Qa5+ (this was the point of 5...e5, but...) 7 Bd2 Qxe5 8 0-0-0!! Nxe4 (8...Qxe4 9 Re1 wins the queen)

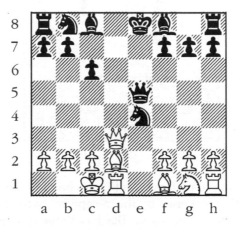

9 Qd8+!! Kxd8 10 Bg5+ Kc7 (10...Ke8 allows another mate in one with 11 Rd8) 11 Bd8 mate! (R.Réti-S.Tartakower, Vienna 1910).

Other choices suggested by young students after **1 e4 c6 2 d4 d5 3 Nc3 dxe4 4 Nxe4** included the enticing **4...f5?**.

(see following diagram)

This move certainly gains time by attacking the knight and also fights for control of the e4-square. However, it can be compared to the move 6...c5?! after 1 e4 e5 2 Nf3 Nc6 3 Nc3 Nf6 4 d4 cxd4 5 Nxd4 Nxd4 6 Qxd4 (see page 84) in that it has more than one negative feature and these certainly outweigh the positives:

1) It weakens the black king.

2) It blocks the development route for Black's light-squared bishop on c8.

3) It leaves White with a potential outpost on e5.

4) It leaves the e7-pawn backward and vulnerable down the half-open e-file.

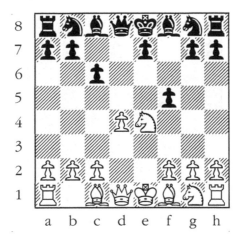

4...e6 prepares to develop the f8-bishop, but the flipside is that its partner on c8 is blocked in. That's why theory prefers ...Bf5 and only then ...e7-e6.

If Black were looking for another way to solve the bishop problem then 4...g6!?,

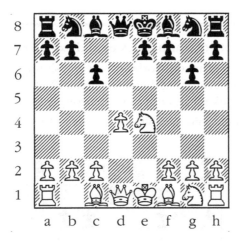

preparing a fianchetto, is logical because this leaves the c8-h3 diagonal open.

Finally I should mention 4...Nd7, which I'll look at in Chapter 6.

4) 1 e4 c5 2 Nf3 d5? 3 exd5 Qxd5 is not a good line for Black because White can gain time on the queen with 4 Nc3 and Black is in danger of slipping seriously behind on development.

In contrast, 2 c3 d5 3 exd5 Qxd5 is a common move order.

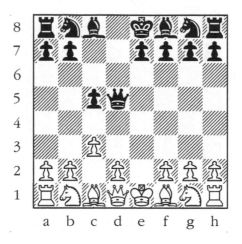

The crucial difference here is that White's c2-c3 has deprived him of the immediate option of Nc3, and Black's queen is more stable on the d5-square (see Chapter 5 for more about this line).

Chapter Five

1) 3...Nf6! and 3...d5!, both of which attack e4 and exploit the weakness of 3 c3.

2) 9 Nh4! is a strong move, not only offering the possibility of Qh5+ (this is a threat) and Nf5, but also preparing the pawn break f2-f4 which would automatically activate White's rook on f1. Let's look at a couple of lines:

a) 9...g6 (preventing both Qh5+ and Nf5) 10 f4! exf4 11 Bxf4.

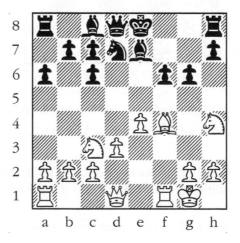

Now White has no need to worry about the forking 11...g5? due to 12 Qh5+! Kf8 13 Bxg5 – the rook on f1 is already working!

b) After 9...0-0, 10 Nf5 is enticing, but there's nothing wrong with the immediate 10 f4!. Following 10...exf4 11 Bxf4...

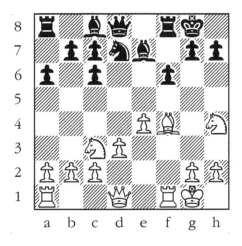

...it seems Black can win a piece with 11...g5 but after 12 Nf5! capturing on f4 gets mated: 12...gxf4 13 Qg4+ Kh8 14 Qg7; or 13...Kf7 14 Nh6+! Ke8 15 Qh5+ Rf7 16 Qxf7.

3) Not at all. Following 5 Bxd6 cxd6!...

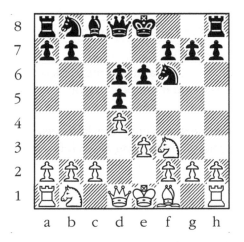

...the doubled d-pawns are in no way vulnerable and they cover some very important central squares. In particular, White no longer has the option of occupying e5 with the knight. In fact, White commonly declines to trade on d6 and prefers to play 5 Bg3!. Now it's Black who has to think twice about exchanging: after 5...Bxg3 White recaptures towards the centre and gives his rook a useful half-open file with 6 hxg3!.

Glossary

castling long

Castling on the queenside.

castling short

Castling on the kingside.

desperado

The act of causing as much disruption as possible with a piece that is already doomed.

diagonal

A diagonal row of squares; the line on which a bishop moves.

discovered attack

This occurs when a piece moves off a line (a file, rank or diagonal), uncovering an attack from another piece behind it on the same line.

discovered check

This is a special version of the discovered attack. It occurs when a piece moves off a line (a file, rank or diagonal), uncovering a check from another piece behind it on the same line.

double check

This is a special version of the discovered check. It occurs when a piece moves off a line (a file, rank or diagonal) to give check, uncovering another check from a different piece behind it on the same line.

en prise

Under attack. One might say 'I blundered and left my queen en prise.'

exchange

When both sides capture pieces, usually of the same value. For example, one might say 'we exchanged rooks.' Confusingly, 'the exchange' is also used when one player wins a rook for a minor piece. This player 'wins the exchange'.

FIDE

Fédération Internationale des Échecs (the World Chess Federation).

file

A line of squares travelling vertically up the board.

fool's mate

1 f3? e5 2 g4?? Qh4 mate!

fork

An attack on more than one enemy piece or pawn.

Fritz

A very popular commercial chess computer engine.

gambit

An opening where one player offers to give up material, usually to obtain an attack of some sort.

grandmaster

A chess player of the highest class.

hanging

En prise.

illegal move

A move that is not permitted by the rules of the game. For example, moving a king into check is illegal.

Kasparov, Garry

Arguably the strongest and most famous figure in chess history.

kingside

The area of the board consisting of all the squares on the e-, f-, g- and h-files.

legal move

A move that is permitted by the rules of the game.

line

A file, rank or diagonal.

major piece

A queen or a rook.

mate

This is shorthand for checkmate.

middlegame

The phase of the game that follows the opening.

minor piece

A bishop or a knight.

patzer

A poor player.

pin

An attack on a piece that cannot move off the line of attack without exposing a more valuable piece behind it.

perpetual check

An unstoppable series of check that usually signals a draw.

queenside

The area of the board consisting of all the squares on the a-, b-, c- and d-files.

rank

A line of squares travelling horizontally across the board.

sacrifice

A move that deliberately gives up material for other gains; to make such a move,

skewer

An attack on a piece that cannot move off the line of attack without exposing a piece of equal or less value behind it.

simultaneous display

A number of games played at the same time by one player against several opponents.

tempo

A unit of time; a move. You might say, 'I gained a tempo by attacking his queen.'

trade

Another word for exchange.

unpin

To break a pin.

zwischenzug

An in-between move; an interpolation during a series of apparently forced moves.

Index of Openings

Lightning Source UK Ltd.
Milton Keynes UK
UKHW011250111218
333774UK00003B/122/P